Five Hour Pilgrim

The right of Tom Cottrell to be identified as the author of this work has been asserted in accordance with the Copyright, Designs and Patents Act, 1988

First published in 2005 by Guide Book Publications, P.O. Box 1236, Parklands, Johannesburg, South Africa. Website: www.runnersguide.co.za

ISBN 0-9584761-9-5

Typeset by Creda Communications in 12 on 15 point Palatino Roman

Cover photographs supplied by
Great Stock Images and Comrades Marathon Association

Cover design by Alan Chaitel — Uptown Design

Printed by Creda Communications

Five Hour Pilgrim

Tom Cottrell

The philosophical meanderings of a nobody

Dear Barrie

Best wishes

Tom Cottrell

, Nov '05.

Dedication

The dedication of a book should only be done after much introspection and soul searching. It is not a thing that is lightly undertaken, and it has great meaning. This book is dedicated to two people. Firstly, I dedicate it to Tiffany Dalton, a close family friend who died of a drug overdose a week after I finished writing the first draft. She died just before her nineteenth birthday, but she didn't have to. Secondly, I dedicate this book to Alison Lowry, Tiffany's mother. She was the person who gave me more than just the impetus to write this book. Alison, may you find the courage to run your race.

Acknowledgements and thanks

You are reading this not only because I wrote it, but also because I had many companions, running partners and coaches. In the first instance, I cannot express my gratitude to Dr Dorian Haarhoff in terms that have sufficient weight. He was a mentor to me in many ways. This book would not have found its proper voice were it not for his patient guidance.

Editing is a sensitive and artistic process in itself, and for this I must thank Kathleen Bartels of Wordsmiths. She displayed keen insight and was at times ruthless, but always highly professional.

The story of Antarctica was helped along in authenticity and detail by the Travel section of the *Saturday Star*. The Maori translations come from *Tikanga Maori — Living by Maori Values*, by Hirini Moko Mead.

I also give thanks to the management board and staff at Hospice-in-the-West. They were a source of inspiration and support that knew no boundary.

Finally, a word of acknowledgement and thanks to my family. My daughters Megan and Bronwyn have been my whole life, my sustenance and my focus. This is a love letter to you both. To my best friend, Kay. After thirty years of marriage, it seems as if there is little more to say. I think not; our conversation has barely begun and I thank you for giving me a life of joy.

"It is not the critic who counts: not the man who points out how the strong man stumbles or where the doer of deeds could have done better. The credit belongs to the man who is actually in the arena, whose face is marred by dust and sweat and blood, who strives valiantly, who errs and comes up short again and again, because there is no effort without error or shortcoming, but who knows the great enthusiasms, the great devotions, who spends himself for a worthy cause; who, at the best, knows, in the end, the triumph of high achievement, and who, at the worst, if he fails, at least he fails while daring greatly, so that his place shall never be with those cold and timid souls who knew neither victory nor defeat."

Theodore Roosevelt, speech at the Sorbonne, Paris, April 23, 1910

Before we start running ...

When my first book, *The Runners' Guide to Road Races in South Africa* was published, my ego knew no boundaries. Truthfully, it was hardly a work of art or literature. More a compilation of facts, badly bound between two covers. Still, my dream had come true. I had written a book and it was there for all to see on the bookshelves. You could even buy a copy if you so desired.

With Border collie excitement and pent-up ego, I called my good friend, Alison Lowry, managing director of Penguin Books in South Africa. Alison was a published writer like myself. Well, to put us in the same marathon would be a long stretch of the imagination; she had written fiction, and talks were underway to have some of her books serialised for TV. My offering was a far cry from this level of publishing, but I was unstoppable.

She graciously met with me and extended to me all the courtesy our friendship would allow.

"Alison, I would like to write a philosophical book on road running. Something that gets into the mind and the soul of a runner. Now that I have my first book out, I'll give you first bite of the apple — what do you say?"

Alison took a long, hard look at me and sat back in her chair. An eternity of silence passed, the clock ticked, the cups rattled, and finally she spoke.

"Tom, I'm not sure about this."

I looked at a caption she had framed on her wall, directly in her line of vision. It read: "Yes — but will it SELL?"

"To be brutally frank" she said, "I'm not sure that anyone really wants to read the philosophical meanderings of a nobody ..."

The conversation was over.

I have forgiven Alison and our friendship is as strong as ever. But it could have been over if my ego had got in the way.

The philosophical meanderings of a nobody? Well then, that is it. I closed the door behind me ... nice title for a book. Well, maybe a sub-title.

Whatever is held on these pages, it is philosophical. It is also a story of a runner. A nobody? Well you, gentle reader, will be the judge of that.

Contents

CHAPTER 1

Prologue to a Pilgrimage

——o0o——

"You kicked me again you little bugger. You really are getting stroppy today, aren't you?"

When Dot came home that evening, she was mildly irritable. The lift in her apartment block had been out-of-order for more than a week and she had had to climb two flights of stairs, yet again. Quietly cursing Jarvis, the building superintendent, she made a mental note to write a strongly worded letter before the sun set. She was laden with the week's groceries and six months pregnant. Add to that a hot December afternoon and the gin and tonic at the office Christmas lunch — the lift would have been welcome.

She struggled up the stairs and fumbled her way forward, opening the door to the kitchen. There were small beads of perspiration on her forehead. She wondered if married life and motherhood was really for her. Life had seemed less complicated and she had enjoyed more freedom before she met Darkey. She loved him, but in her make-up she was a career girl. Somewhere deep inside her were tiny seeds of resentment. Life would change for her in ways she could not yet fathom. Uncharted water, Dottie, this is all uncharted water.

She opened the fridge, put in the perishables and took a long swig from a bottle of Coke. She was beginning to feel a bit better. Then she went into the flat in search of her soul mate, the father of her child — Darkey. She flung open the passage door with arms outstretched and a "te-dah". In that moment it was strange how the detail rushed in at her. The clock on the mantelpiece struck the quarter-hour, there was an ashtray with five cigarette butts, and faintly in the distance she could hear the summer call of a *piet-my-vrou*. A sure sign that it would rain that night. Her mouth dropped open and she fell to her knees ...

Dot had made Thomas chase her for two years before she would let him marry her. All his friends knew Thomas as "Darkey". He had unusually dark features for a Welshman. He was 14 years older than her and there were times when she thought he was just a silly old man. But Darkey was passionate, mad about this lively woman who simply oozed fun and laughter, to the point of being reckless.

"I will pursue you to the ends of the earth," he declared. "You are the one for me, and there is no escape."

The clincher happened one early morning when, just before sunrise, he stood outside Dot's bedroom window and loudly confessed his love for her. Putting on his best drunken-sailor act, holding onto a lamp pole, he sang to her and then proposed on bended knee in the street. Many of the other residents were not amused at the pre-dawn intrusion, but Dot would always treasure that moment.

In early March 1953 Dot and Darkey married. She worked in the accounts department at Kodak. He, a bricklayer by trade, took an office job with the city council as a building inspector. A happy couple. Dot loved Darkey's absurd sense of humour and fun.

He loved to surprise her when she came home from work. One evening in early June, Darkey prepared an elaborate scene for Dot's return. Edmund Hillary had climbed Everest the month before. Darkey piled pillows; cushions and anything else he could find into a mountain on their ample bed. He placed himself on the summit, complete with bomber-jacket, flying cap and goggles from his Air Force days in North Africa. With British flag in one hand, a bottle of champagne in the other, mayhem and laughter greeted Dot. Later that night, amid scattered cushions, pillows and howls of laughter, Dot fell pregnant.

A cigarette butt still smouldered in the ashtray. Darkey's body was still warm, but Dot knew he was dead. Her initial reaction was one of disbelief: "NO, NO — come on Darks — wake up."

The dead, staring eyes and limp arm were real. The man who had relentlessly pursued her, the man who sang to her, made her laugh, and was the father of her unborn child was dead in her arms. Dot let out a wail in the still evening air. How could a widow bring up a child? She thought about having an abortion. Somewhere in the swirling background the clock on the mantelpiece struck the half-hour.

All the people from the city council attended Darkey's funeral. He was greatly loved, and it came as a pleasant, yet melancholy, surprise to Dot just how many of his colleagues revered the dark Welshman. In a final salute, the local Welsh Choir offered a stirring rendition of *Bread of Heaven*. There wasn't a dry eye in the house when the pallbearers slow-marched out of the packed church to *Danny Boy*.

In the pew, there was a lively kick.

"I know, I know. Now just sit still, the service is almost over."

Kodak turned out in full force, even the MD, Mr Field, was there. After the service he put his expansive arms around Dot. "Don't worry Dottie — we'll look after you." Mr Field kept his word.

All Darkie's fellow ex-servicemen from "up North" were at the noisy wake, as were the members of their bowling club. Widowhood had not yet made its unwelcome and lonely presence felt. For the moment Dot was brave at the grave, and was the perfect, if slightly tipsy, hostess at her husband's last party.

Heartbroken, Dot moved back home with her parents. She could not live in the flat alone. Her life was now an empty promise. Her pregnancy was nearing the end. Soon the backache and unbearable heat would be a thing of the past. It was a new year and the baby was due in early March.

Dot finally began to grieve for the loss of her love. The management at Kodak was empathetic and understanding, and Dot did not return to work. She sat alone in her room and wept.

"What is to become of us?" she would ask her unborn child. It was a month until the baby was due. "What is to become of us?"

February 1954 passed agonisingly for Dot. Sometimes she could not believe that she would never see Darkey again. At times her life was a blur and she would drink just a bit too much gin to take off the painful edge. Dot's life was beginning to unravel and so was she. The worst were the long nights when, in the dark, depression would set in. In this void she would cling to her unborn child and cry.

In the mornings she would wake in anger. Angry that her child would not have a father — especially a father like Darkey. Rocking back and forth, she cried, "Oh, what is to become of us?"

The process of losing your love is a lonely and dark road.

Dot dreaded the coming of her child. Although it was late February, and still summer, she could sense a chill in the air, and even the leaves looked tired as they clung to the last hope of warm, balmy evenings.

She was ill-prepared for childbirth, and shocked when her waters broke. Her father, never cool under pressure, went into a panic. It was late in the evening, and thankfully, there was no rush-hour traffic on the way to the hospital. They managed as a family to pack a suitcase for Dot and find the car keys. Amidst much shouting, swearing and confusion they got her to the maternity ward at the Florence Nursing Home in Hillbrow.

Dot stared up at the lights in the theatre. It was cold and the people around her were strangers. The pain was unbearable and she shut her eyes tightly. "Oh God, Oh Darkey ... what is to become of us? How will I survive without you?" Outside, the city was beginning to wake up. Dawn was breaking and a bird began to sing.

Confusion, pain, more confusion. "Here it comes ... It's a boy ... Congratulations. Shall we clean him up first?"

Dot looked at her son for the first time. He had a shock of black hair and his eyes were dark. So small. She studied him. All the parts were there and in working order. "He looks just like his father," Dot thought. "You have been with me through all of this — you have no father, he died. I'm sorry."

She looked at him, now sleeping in her arms. Then the small bundle woke, opened his eyes and yawned, squirmed, and went back to sleep. For the first time since Darkey's death, Dot felt a deep sense of calm. "I shall name you Thomas."

* * *

I put down the pair of my mother's shoes I was holding. I was consumed by an empty, haunting sadness. The room was stark, the apartment empty. I was too young and inexperienced to deal with such loss. Life was so unfair. My mother's funeral was fresh in my mind and here I was cleaning out her possessions before the new tenants moved in. With a fresh coat of paint, the fragrance of a woman's being would be expunged from this empty shell.

Dot had so looked forward to her retirement; to her "pension days" as she called them. Each month she would buy something special — a new pair of "pension shoes" or a "retirement read" — to store away for those glorious days, when she could kick back and relax, and not have go to the office. She had worked all her life, and her "pension days" were to be days of bliss and peace.

She and Hilda Strang, a woman of similar age who worked in the accounts department with her, had their retirement all planned out. They would take a trip to the coast for a month in celebration. The best thing about it would be that they wouldn't even need to fill out a leave form for their pompous manager, Reginald. They would just go.

When the first shock wave hit her, she knew something was terribly wrong. It started as a pain in the centre of her chest that would not go away. This was more than just a bout of indigestion. Her left arm was numb, and she knew she needed help. She crawled to the phone on her hands and knees. Scared, she hoped she could remember the number. She dialled, sweating. The pain was unbearable. It was late, but she didn't care, this was an emergency. The phone clicked, someone picked up ...

"Hello," said a sleepy voice. "Tom speaking ..."

* * *

I kneel on the floor, and emptiness and sadness overwhelms me. I have packed up dozens of pairs of shoes that have never been worn, dresses with price tags still attached. Unread books. Even a set of children's books bought for her unborn grandchildren. What a waste of a life,

I thought. My mother put her entire life, still with its wrapping paper and price tag, into the cupboard. She was hardly concerned with the precious moment before her. Rather she traded all of that for an unrealistic promise that was never to be. She would never read those books in her retirement, never would those shoes feel the soft warmth of beach sand. She held back her joy and spontaneity for a day that would never come.

I invited most of Dot's old friends to help themselves to her clothes. They came and paraded, strutted and squabbled over my mother's "pension day" dream, like vultures to the carcass. I recalled a bizarre scene in the movie *Zorba the Greek*, where the villagers stripped a dead woman's dwelling. All that was left in the end was a lonely corpse in the middle of a bare floor.

As I handed the key to Mr Jaffe, the caretaker, and drove away from my mother's apartment for the last time, I made a promise to myself: I will live in the moment. I will not put off the pleasures of today for some other time, for some other event. When the sun rises, I will meet it at its rising, and as it sets, I will rejoice in the evening. When love is given to me, I will accept it without question.

I will look to the future, but never at the expense of the present moment. I will trust what is before me, in the here and now. And every time I don a pair of running shoes, to go out on a training run or a race, I will think of my mother. My shoes will be well run-in.

The clothes in my cupboard will be worn, and some may even be threadbare. The books on my shelf will be read; well-thumbed and marked where there are passages of wisdom or love.

Wine is there for the drinking; food is there for the eating. The people in my life are there for the loving. My daily work is there for my challenge and my growth, and my wife is there for me to adore. Not at some time in the future, but here, now, in the fullness of the day.

* * *

It is late in the afternoon as I sit alone in my study and try to come to grips with my life. I am approaching my fiftieth year and I feel a strong compulsion to write something. No matter how ordinary a life may seem, it is never so ordinary that it should go unrecorded. And so I begin these philosophical meanderings; a love letter of sorts.

These writings are an expression of my life, my spirit. I have decided that my fiftieth year will be a milestone event. I will embark on a journey of self-discovery. I want to make re-acquaintance with my Soul, in such need of repair.

I hold my family in my mind. My wife, Kay. My daughters, Megan and Bronwyn. I sit them down and explain that I want to spend my fiftieth year on a private pilgrimage. Patiently, puzzled, they hear me out: "As I take to the road, I can only tell you that I love you, that I always have done; and I would, in a blink, give my life unconditionally for each of you. In truth I have given it already. What is mine, even my life itself, is yours."

Never weep over unexpressed feelings, never regret unworn shoes, unread books, they are not my mistakes. But I have a journey to go on. Let me depart, for the tide is in my favour.

* * *

Tap, tap, tap. "One, two, one, two."

I sit nervously in the studio of a radio station. A sound engineer bustles behind a glass panel in a separate room, and I fiddle to get my headset to work. Deep breathing now, Tom, deep breathing. I just love the direct, business-like feel of radio. I feel important.

Outside the soundproof studio window, I look over the

evening panorama of Johannesburg as the sun sets behind Northcliff Hill. Five stories below there is silent mayhem in the streets. Here, in this dimly lit cocoon, there is focus and intent, as the clock ticks to the hour.

"Thirty seconds," announces the engineer. Throats clear and I look across at the Sporttime interviewer, Terry Jack. "Five, four, three, two, one ... on air!"

"Good evening, listeners, we have author, publisher and teacher Tom Cottrell in the studio tonight, and he is doing something very different with his running this year. He is going on a pilgrimage. Tell the listeners, Tom, what sort of pilgrimage is this?" As interviewers go, Terry Jack is good. He is insightful and knows how to open up the conversation.

"A pilgrimage is a journey to a holy place, to commemorate a past event, or as a celebration or an act of penance. The goal may be a sacred river or mountain; the location of a miracle, revelation or theophany; or even the tomb of a hero or saint."

"Tom, you don't strike me as a pilgrim type?"

"True. This will be a pilgrimage of a different kind, it will certainly be a celebration, but it is more than that."

To give the listeners more background, I start at the beginning. "My father died before I was born."

I see Terry leaning forward now.

"That is important in itself, but there are two essentials here. The first is that I was born with an innate understanding of suffering and of tragedy. I was literally within my mother's grief. It was my reality and I knew that this secret wisdom would be with me from birth and for all my living days. Secondly, my father died of a heart attack, at a relatively young age, and I have already outlived him."

I see Terry shuffling his papers, getting ready with a question. But I need to explain properly, I hold up my hand and plough on. "My mother also died of a heart attack early in her life. So both my parents left me with a genetic weakness. That could mean I have a relatively short shelf-life. This is a pilgrimage more of celebration than anything else. Before I die I want to make a contribution, I want to see the world, and I want to have some fun."

This is the year I turn fifty. A milestone. A special year. The perfect time in my life for a pilgrimage. I am strong physically and still athletic. I have been around the block a few times; I have some wisdom and understanding, even some knowledge.

I can take the gap now because my children are almost grown up and independent. They had a private school education, they are both at university, and they both have straight teeth. Do you have any idea how much all of that costs? How much fatherly dedication it entails? Now, for the first time in my life, I am going to do something for myself.

"So what sort of pilgrimage is this?"

"Well, Terry ..." — Nice one, boykie, giving me lots of room to talk.

"I love running long distances. I have even written books on the subject, it's a passion of mine. So here's the plan — I want to run a marathon on every continent in my fiftieth year. To my mind the last ten kilometres of any marathon is a holy place, a place where the mind and the spirit leave the body and soar to another dimension. The marathon race is a pilgrimage. Not only do I want to run these marathons, I also want to celebrate being a citizen of the world."

"I believe that success or failure in a race, as in life, is a measure of our moral fibre. In those magical miles, the miles of truth, we are stripped bare of the false titles and privileges that society bestows on us. Here, a rich man's wallet only weighs him down. Material wealth means nothing. The race cares little for the rank that money can buy. In such a place, hard work is what matters. It is to this place that I want to make my pilgrimage."

"But Tom, you broke your leg several years ago — do you think you'll be up to it?"

I admire an interviewer who has done his homework.

"I did break my leg in a car accident several years ago, and when I run, I do so in pain. But most runners are hurting at the end of a marathon, so I'm in good company. My brother-in-law died in that accident. For me to participate is more like a celebration. The pain affirms that there is still life in me.

"Part of this pilgrimage is a journey into my own Soul. It may well be that I have to embark on it as an act of penance for the guilt I feel for the death of my brother-in-law. If that is true, then many elements are present to make this a sacred journey of body, mind and spirit.

"But there is more to this than simply going on a running jaunt around the world. I want to make a contribution to the world. I want to make a difference."

"Like campaign for world peace?" asks Terry.

Flippant bastard, but I won't be put off my stride.

"No Terry, something real, something tangible. You see, death has been my running companion. I am a trained Hospice counsellor. I give emotional support to terminal patients. This voluntary work comes with all the feelings and understanding I have as an only child who lost his parents early on."

"I want to raise money for Hospice. If possible, I want to serve on the management committee for a while. Get ideas so that I can learn more about what the real needs are."

"Charity work is not about paying money over to an organisation to ease or soothe your guilt. Real charity work is about involvement, and the most precious gift you can give is yourself and your time. If I'm on the management board I can see that projects are followed through." I feel I must emphasise the point. "Charity is about involvement and commitment, like the whole of life. If it isn't, rather don't do it."

And there is more, I explain to the patient interviewer. I want to write a book.

Terry looks up.

It is a birthday present to myself. I have appointed a mentor, a great man, a professor of English and philosophy to help me with this quest. I don't want my life to go unrecorded. I want to make a statement. I want something tangible that expresses my love.

"So tell me Tom, do you expect to sell many copies of this book, then?" The inevitable question.

"If I make only three copies for my wife and two daughters, and staple them together, it will be enough. I care little for its commercialisation. It's a love letter, Terry. How can you put a value on that?"

"Tom, with all due respect, it is madness." Terry launches forth about wandering around in the desert on a meaningless quest. Strolling about with madmen. "Tom don't you think ..." I become angry, a good time to interrupt.

"No, definitely not Terry, no way. These are not just the philosophical meanderings of a middle-aged fart, of a nobody; this is serious stuff. It's an attempt at finding out who I am and what I can achieve."

The bath water is cold. I look up at the ceiling and remove my heel from the plughole. A last clockwise gurgle. The water has run out of my bath as I hold the plug to my mouth. Time has run out. Above me the radio plays the signature tune for the News at Eight.

This is madness, I think. Why go to all this trouble, and for what? I step out of the bath and dry myself off.

"Ah well, onward and upward into the day." Terry Jack will join me at bath time tomorrow morning and we'll finish the interview then.

CHAPTER 2

Dumping the Files

—o0o—

"Do you want your tie?"

I was holding Neels' tie in my hand.

"What the hell are you doing? Leave my tie alone!"

I repeated the question.

"Yes, of course I do. Now leave me alone — you are in big trouble, you know."

I surprised myself; I was so calm. A pair of scissors lay on the desk. I grabbed, cut and threw his tie in his lap.

"There, there is your frigging tie — now I resign. The rest of the paperwork I'll finish tomorrow. Oh, I'll leave my car keys with Sharon at reception."

"Christ, what are you doing Tom?" I thought as I walked out of Neels' office. The child in me was punching the air in victory. "Yes, yes, yes. You showed that son-of-a-bitch."

A dramatic climax to almost twenty years of being a poor corporate citizen. I started out my working life as a young, bright accountant bursting with new ideas and hugely over-ambitious. Way beyond my abilities. But I was unstoppable.

On the long and sometimes futile path that was my "professional life", this corporate camel has been stabbed in the back, passed over for promotion, and retrenched. Neels was the final straw. There is a saying: "Leave all things to Allah, but tie up your camel". This outburst was not done entirely out of context. I had already made arrangements elsewhere, I just really felt I had to make my point to yet another boss who was like all the rest — an insane sycophant with no boundary around a bloated ego. Wisdom would later teach me that this was more about my own abrasiveness and stupidity.

That is how I became a shareholder in a publishing company and also the MD. With one snip of a corporate tie, I became a big deal. I also became a writer and publisher. Halfway through my life I found my release.

I busied myself with work I was passionate about. For the first time in more than a decade, I was doing something important in my working life. The company grew; I began to prosper. A partner was brought in and we started to employ more people. A holding company held the majority of shares, and I had to bow to their wishes from time to time. But for the time being, I didn't care. I was the maker of my own destiny. I was so busy building a company that I failed to look out of the window and see the dark clouds on the horizon.

I was the last in the company to know that the axe was about to fall. Everyone had been briefed, except me. All plans were tentatively in place. Conversations suddenly stopped when I walked into a huddled gathering of my colleagues. Even the small talk became, well, small. Eye contact, now a rare commodity, was replaced by wistful looks, often misinterpreted. Had I been more astute, more honest, I would have picked up the warning signs months before. I would have seen the sympathy in the looks, more importantly I would have understood that many were living in fear. Fear for their own circumstances.

When you have surrendered more than two decades of your working life to corporate comfort and safety, it is all too frightening to face the truth. More than simple security, I was about to lose all my ambitions, my hopes and all I wanted from a working life.

The board meeting had gone well. We had planned strategies, the chairman made notes, nodding and smiling throughout. Lunch was ordered in, and all through the afternoon we plotted and planned around the boardroom table. We saw the pot of gold at the end of the rainbow, all we had to do was go and get it. We knew what we wanted, and this was a meeting of strategy. No blue-sky gazing.

Afterwards the chairman folded his notes and said he had an important announcement. It was a warm summer's afternoon. Our offices were in a garden park, and one could hear the birds busying themselves as they put themselves and their families to bed. The evening was setting in and a warm breeze blew through the window and carried with it the evening scents of the Highveld.

It was suddenly quiet, and I watched the chairman compose himself for the big moment. "There will have to be a general retrenchment. As from Monday everybody in the company will have to go. We are closing you down. I am sorry."

The silence that followed could have lasted a second, a minute ... an hour. I am not sure. One thing that did remain were the feelings. My back went cold; my thoughts went into neutral, and time stood still. I do not remember what the chairman said next. I do remember driving home in a daze. Peak-hour traffic, but I might as well have been driving on an empty road. My life had shrunk and closed up into a cocoon, about the size of the car.

I was dazed. During the next two days I swept my driveway. I somehow had to tell my family. I needed their support. I had the weekend, but what was I to do on Monday morning? Pretend that I was going to work? Not an option. How was I going to explain this to my young children, not yet in their teens?

I chose dinnertime to break the news. How do I explain that all I have ever worked for and all of my ambitions have been taken away? How do I explain hardship? We may lose our house, and a life we have become accustomed to.

I wanted to tell them of my anger, and I wanted them to understand my fear. How to do this? I feared the loss of their respect, even their love. I felt that I had failed them. I drew a deep breath and began. I had to deal with my dwindling self-esteem. I had been rejected by the corporate pile. I looked into expectant faces: "I hope that you won't reject me too."

I told them in the simplest and most truthful way. All listened quietly. For the first time, this young family, my family, found new dimensions. There was silence when I needed to pause and reflect. I was still afraid, but I knew that we had a future because of the love and unity at that table.

My youngest daughter, Bronwyn, broke that silence. "Dad, I was at the shopping centre today, and outside Smiley Blue there was a sign on the window that said they wanted a shop assistant. I know you could do that job, Dad. Go down tomorrow and ask them for the job."

I reflected on what Bronwyn had said. Something powerful was beginning to stir within me. I could not articulate it then, but I knew she was right about something. At four the next morning Kay was pacing the floor and fretting. "What are we going to do? We have two children to educate, a huge bond on this house, and our cars are not even paid for. What will happen to us?" I lay awake too, but I knew a way forward.

I drew on the power that my youngest daughter had displayed at the dinner table. "Sit down, Kay. Stop your worrying, it's futile."

Easy words to be sure, but for the next hour I explained what was going on in my mind. "Worry is the enemy, worry is debilitating. We can consume ourselves, expend energy and yet, sadly, nothing will have changed. Worry is wasteful. You can spend ten percent of your time on worry, for that is normal and natural. The rest of the time, the ninety percent, you work with me here. We will build a future and we will survive, that is my promise to you."

We held each other in that cool dawn, and watched the sun rise. I felt afraid of the future, that was the honest truth. But I would proceed with the mind of a distance runner. One step at a time, I would run this race.

I learned a lot as I lived through the next few days. Sadly there are few helpful books on retrenchment. Besides, most have been written by consultants with an academic and passing interest in the subject, who, because of their vast knowledge, are able to write on being out of work. Others who wrote on the subject were employed, probably had never been retrenched, and knew how they would be paying the mortgage next month.

I had to map the route as I went along.

I did a number of things right. I established a support base early on. I engaged my family. Plans were made, suggestions put forward. "I'll give up my pocket money, Dad." God, how I loved my children for their input. I was not alone. This, at a time when my self-confidence and self-esteem was under attack from within. A time when my emotions rose and bubbled to the surface. But here was a safe place, where I could deal with my own negativity.

Out of a job after more than twenty years. I was middle-aged and felt betrayed. I was a pale male in Africa. Self-doubt, low self-esteem and anger. The loss was of the same magnitude as a death.

The cycle of emotion is the same, no matter what the loss. That feeling of numbness in the place where time stands still. Then the phase of denial. "This isn't happening to me, all will be fine." I kept repeating this to myself while I dumbly swept my garage floor. Once I got through the anger and the fear, I became depressed. I felt inadequate. But it is here that real growth takes place, and I knew it.

I told my bank manager the news. Strangely, I found him sympathetic. I asked about rescheduling my debts, I asked him to look with sympathy on already strained finances. He was an employee as well, with his own objectives. But he did pledge his support and that was good enough for me.

I also told my friends, business associates and anyone who cared to listen. To my amazement, I found a groundswell of support, which was a great morale booster. While few, if any, were forthcoming with material help, I knew that I had an encouraging crowd lining the uphill route.

I fantasised about how I would exact my revenge on my boss. Publicly humiliate him, hire hit men, burn his house down, wreck his car. Have him arrested and thrown into jail. Would I be satisfied, would I feel justice had been done? I was unsure. I might feel satisfied for a short while, but I would remain jobless. It became clear in my musings about his fate that I would still, after all, be in the same predicament. It was an enlightening moment.

I resolved to shake the dust of this desire from my running shoes. "Living well" I once read, "is the best revenge". That is how I would spend my thinking time, positive and focused. But I had to run through the desert of revenge before I got to this oasis. In the end I sued the chairman and his cronies. One against five, I had them completely surrounded.

* * *

"Beware of those on whose heads you stand on the way up, for verily you shall meet those same people on the way down." A colleague once shared this wisdom with me in the canteen. In some way or other, everyone who has ever worked has felt the icy chill of the knife blade, called betrayal, go in. Right from the time the carpenters busied themselves building Noah's Ark, office politics has played its cruel hand on the unsuspecting.

Errol sat across the table from me with his hands folded. He looked nervous. I hadn't seen him since the court case. He was one of the directors who had tripped up this runner. Now he was a salesman. I was the owner of my own business. How desperately did he need this commission?

I had conducted my own case and was meticulous in the gathering of information, documents and knowledge. Errol and his board members underestimated my resolve, and misguided, they arrived at the hearing with only a handful of papers. I walked into the hearing with four lever-arch files bursting with documents and financial records. There was going to be a slaughter.

I was proud of those files, the ones I had assembled for the hearing. As the day wore on, Errol and the other board members became intimidated by the sheer weight of my evidence against them, my presentation, and the intensity of my preparation.

After a satisfactory settlement, I locked these files in a cupboard. They became a trophy. Every now and then I would pull them out and browse through the paper work to remind myself of how unjustly I had been treated, and how righteous was my cause.

Now it was my turn. I explained to Errol "I can't do business with you or the company you represent because of the lack of trust that exists between us." He looked crestfallen. Yes! Revenge! I concluded the meeting as civilly as I could and sat in my office in a daze.

"What has become of me?" I wondered. I went into the files that I had meticulously compiled and flipped, blankly, through the pages. "What has become of me?"

I did not want to become like Errol. I realised that to free myself from all of the "Errols", I had to let them go. The legal files in my hand represented much more than just a victory over a bunch of rogues. These files were like a stone in my shoe, which I did not want to dig out.

I knew what I had to do. I pushed the files into two shopping bags and drove to the local rubbish dump. There, after a small ritual and a prayer, I threw them, lever-arch and all, onto the dump and drove home. I had a bath and resolved never to think of what was held in those files again.

It was a moment of truth, liberation. I thought I might phone Errol and tell him what I had done, but I needed more space to cope with that. In my mind and in my spirit I had been released, I had forgiven, and I had moved on. Through this symbolic act, I learned a lesson. When someone deliberately hurts me, double-crosses me, what is the right response? Do nothing. My life is too full of purpose to waste my time getting even. Life has too much in it to be small.

There will always be people who drain my energy — suck up the oxygen in the room. Over-officious administrators. They can be found in sporting bodies, municipal offices and in the ubiquitous licensing department. They suck the joy of living from every space, until there is nothing left but their own collective misery. These universal black holes inhabit the corporate world too.

I wanted liberation from these black holes. In my

imagination, I sent out an invitation to all the people in my life who had caused me pain, undermined me. To my surprise, the list was long. I even dug back into my childhood.

I invited them all to come and join me on a marathon run. During the first half of the race I ran with them, and I ran slowly. I allowed their negative energy to set the pace and I allowed the conversations to revolve around themselves and all the problems they had with me. I allowed them to tell me in turn how much I had disappointed them. How much they disliked me. It was a slow and painful run, but in my mind this was an important race and it would not last forever. I listened patiently and let the negative talk weigh me down. I had no choice but to run with them, bent over by my burden of guilt and anguish.

We laboriously ran to the thirty-two kilometre mark, the real halfway mark — the point where all hope passes and there is only truth left. Now it was my turn to speak.

"I have been running with you to this point. I have listened patiently while you belittled me. But from here you shall all run at my pace, if you can. You shall all be silent and you shall hear me speak." In the black void there was not even a murmur. "From here to the finish line, this is my race. I forgive you all. Each one of you that has caused me pain and anguish — I set you all free." I leaned into a faster pace, and not one responded.

The black hole could not respond, their pace slowed. "Now goodbye, I have no more time for any of you."

"Just who do you think you are?" responded the blackness. "Do you think that you are too good for us?" Clearly a challenge. "We will settle this in court" — a challenge that sounded more like "I'll tell my Mommy on you".

It is silent back there, but I have no illusions about the

running bunch in my wake. They are relentless and they are tireless. If I slacken the pace, even a little, the great black hole will catch up and engulf me.

I have forgiven each negative participant in turn, and allowed them to run at their own pace. From this point on, I run free, and I run easy, without fear. More importantly, I run with love in my heart.

CHAPTER 3

Sally!

———o0o———

Autumn. A time for reflection. As the leaves turn colour and fall from the trees, thoughts leave me melancholy and alone. I think of death, of tragedy. How do I tell this story well? How do I do justice to such a sad passage of life? A few short years before, at this turn of the season, I said goodbye to Sally. I held her hand and softly whispered, "Sally, I will always remember and love you."

She said nothing.

I turned away with a pained heart, and headed for the airport. As I felt the familiar tug of the Jumbo bound for London powering down the runway, my mind was screaming, my emotions in turmoil. This would be our final goodbye. The doctor had pointed that out the day before; and the hissing and gurgling of the machines attached to a body with no soul said it all.

Kay and I were high-school sweethearts and I had known Sally for as long I had known Kay. Kay was the eldest sister of three. Sally was in the middle. She was the one with the good looks and the bright smile. The pick of the three Jones sisters. She carried herself in a way that only beautiful, confident women can. Picky with boyfriends too. Her school sweetheart was a good-looking lad from Finland named Risto Silvennoinen. I thought he was pure, one hundred percent jerk.

Sally and Risto moved in a different social environment to Kay and me. They were the beautiful people who went to sophisticated clubs with exotic-sounding names. Kay and I were Girl Guide and Boy Scout who frequented the Bridgeways Group at the local Methodist Church. We inhabited different planets.

Kay discovered years later there had been some sort of secret conspiracy going on behind her back. Sally would tell her school friends that she had a younger sister, Jenny, but denied any direct blood relationship to her fat, pig-tailed, church-going Girl Guide of an older sister. Frankly, she was an embarrassment.

Risto was in the army doing his year-long national service, and Sally was in her final year of high school. Because I was very close to Kay from an early age, I became very much part of the Jones family. Being an only child and having no real family of my own, they became my family. Sally was like the sister I never had.

The consequence of one of Risto's weekend passes became evident after the final school results came out. Sally was pregnant before she matriculated. She was terrified to tell her father she was pregnant, she was even terrified to tell me! But in the end that is what she did, knowing full well that I would take it to "the family".

Basil, father to Sally, flew into an Anglican rage of self-righteousness and indignation. He was a lay preacher and at times a pompous ass. The rant and rave swung dangerously from questioning the moral character of every Finn ever born, to being a gentle and caring father who understood his daughter's plight.

Betty, Basil's long-suffering and patient wife, was a bustling nursing sister with the no-nonsense bearing of too many years of night-duty. She seemed to live in the shadow of her formidable husband. Perhaps her deafness stifled her interaction with an unsympathetic and sometimes uncaring world. Her approach to the situation was to enfold Sally with empathy and love. She embraced a motherly understanding of her daughter in distress.

There were family discussions about abortion, adoption or keeping the baby. In those years abortion was illegal in South Africa. If this were the choice it would have to be done in London. One thing that was not only left off the table, but also put firmly out of the building and dumped in the car park was the idea of marrying "that slimy Finnish bastard".

This seemed to suit Risto fine at the time. He once had the temerity to venture into the unforgiving territory of "how do you know it's my child?" That of course made Risto, his entire family, and all of Finland slimy and untrustworthy. By the time the baby was born, Risto would have completed his army training and be well into his first year of architecture at Wits University. Why mess up the lives of young people on the verge of a career? Adoption became the most sane and logical option.

Sally was sent to a home in the north of Pretoria for young, unmarried mothers. She settled into the routine and loneliness of a hostel existence. She was brave about her life in the home, but Kay and I could see her heart.

As the birth-date approached, the father needed to sign consent for the adoption. This meant Risto would have to go to the home, see Sally and sign the papers. He was living a great student life and was actively working at putting emotional distance between his life as a respectable, fun-loving student of architecture and that of a cad. It was a responsibility that he wanted to avoid.

Risto was becoming a slippery eel and was living up to the reputation that Basil was trying to label him with. I was the one charged with the task of dragging his sorry ass out of his university flat, frogmarching him to my car, and driving him to the home where Sally was getting more swollen with child every day. I despised Risto for his childish, if not cruel protestations of innocence. The drive to Pretoria was in silence, the drive home took forever.

I cannot even begin to understand the anguish Sally must have felt when she gave up her son. I cannot know what it must have been like to have the warmth, the smell and the comfort of your baby against you, and in one swift movement, have it taken away as papers are stamped, and the child is bundled up and taken to a strange home. No contact for the next twenty-one years. What I *do* know though, is that she never failed to celebrate her first child's birthday. She never forgot. She named him Justin.

I first saw Sally after Justin's birth when she was a bridesmaid to Kay at our wedding. Sally had had part of her soul ripped from her, and even though she still had a vivacious presence, there was a haunting emptiness in her eyes. Few saw it, but she knew I wasn't fooled.

Married life flooded Kay and me as we struggled to build a life. Kay was a teacher and I a cost accountant in a bank, working hard to finish my degree at night school. Risto was at the same university. Sally had opted — or rather pushed — to complete a teaching diploma at a Natal college. We had sporadic contact with her and she would come and stay with us from time to time. Risto had become a bad memory.

Then, the unexpected. News began to filter back to Kay that Sally was making regular, clandestine trips to

Johannesburg to see Risto. Could this be true, after all he had done to her? After a phone call between Kay and Sally it was no longer a secret. Sally started to openly drop by with Risto. She would visit Kay and I in our home while he would wait outside. To my mind, Risto, still the slime-ball in my eyes, was not welcome.

"What is it with Risto?" I would press her. Her answer was simple: Love. This was something that I had to understand. I reluctantly came to the realisation that if we wanted Sally in our lives, Risto would have to be a welcome guest at our table. This was a painful decision.

"If we want to keep Sally," I argued one day with Basil, "we need to embrace Risto."

But how does one go about hugging a slime-ball? I had an idea. Even in the early days of my running, I recognised its healing properties for both body and soul. With all the courage I could muster, I phoned Risto. "Come and run a race with me on Sunday morning." To my surprise, he accepted. The race was on.

While there was nervous and friendly banter in the car on the way to the race, there was savage aggression beneath the smiles. The race would be a hard-fought competition. No quarter given or asked for. Healing properties be damned. This was a show of strength; an all-male charged fight to the death.

From the starter's gun this is exactly what happened. A fast, flat fifteen-kilometre race in Benoni. The intensity of the competition between Risto and me on that day rivalled the most intense fighting in the Somme. In the end, experience — I had run one race before — yielded to youth and Risto beat me by at least two kilometres. Even in my defeat I was elated, I had found a way of engaging "slime-ball" and bringing him into the fold.

It didn't take us long to become knights of the road. Every

Sunday Risto and I set out running races all over Johannesburg, while Kay and Sally prepared a breakfast fit only for great warriors and athletes. We were heroes, and our women patiently prepared for and awaited our return. Every race was the same, Risto beat me by miles, but breakfast and Sunday mornings were developing into pleasant family affairs. My next move would be to get them married.

Risto and I were establishing a workable friendship and we ran well together. Sooner or later we would be running the Comrades Marathon — it was certainly heading that way. Our first marathon, the Johannesburg City Marathon, revealed that while Risto was the undisputed champion of the shorter runs, the long-distance race was my domain. I had his measure. The Comrades would be mine.

By the time we entered our first Comrades, the four of us were two close couples. Risto and I promised to run this great race together, but secretly I had a big score to settle. Risto was still my rival. In the end I beat him by more than an hour. Sweet revenge!

Soon afterwards, Sally and Risto were married. Both Kay and I were ecstatic and I believed the pain of their adopted child would be put behind them. They moved to Umtata, where Risto had a job as an architect and Sally taught at the local primary school.

Building a home, raising children and forging careers flooded our lives. We did not see much of Sally and Risto, but we kept in contact. Our second Comrades Marathon outing was pleasant; the needle was gone. We finished holding hands and spent the evening swearing an uncommon bond, a secret bond between knights of the road. Not long after this their second child was born, another son, the spitting image of his father. They named him Joshua.

We were all excited for Christmas 1989. Kay and I would be at home and Sally would be bringing her newborn son, now three months old, for a long-awaited visit.

But there was a black cloud on the horizon. Sally told Kay that married life was not going well. Risto had been spending a lot of time away from home. This was not in itself out of the ordinary. As a junior partner in his practice he attended many site meetings. They lived in Umtata at a time of rapid apartheid expansion. There were new casinos on the coast and lots of building was going on at the time, creating frenetic energy and attracting contractors, builders suppliers and architects. The inevitable happened. She was very young, attractive and available. He could not resist. And small-town gossip made sure that Risto's infidelity was found out.

I was outraged, I felt personally betrayed. Such an act of deceit would definitely not go unpunished. We were not sure if Risto would be joining us for Christmas lunch but he did show up, arriving with a flourish in his shiny, yellow MG convertible sports car. I poured myself a glass of wine and prepared to do battle.

Lunch was a tense affair given the "elephant in the room". It took me another glass or two of crisp white wine to find my sense of indignation, but once I found it, there was no holding back. I was unstoppable. I gave slime-ball a real working over. Soon the bottles were empty and I was well into my stride. My focus was my own hurt; I did not even notice how uncomfortable everyone else was feeling. "Let's go for a drive, Tom. Let me show you this beauty." Risto tried to break the tension.

Drunk, angry and belligerent, I agreed.

"Don't have an accident." The parting injunction from Kay.

"Don't worry Kay, it's not my car," I said, leaning back in the passenger seat.

Risto and I drove off into the balmy, late Christmas afternoon.

* * *

Kay stood beside me. I recognised the man on the opposite side of the bed as our family doctor. I looked over my body and things slowly came back. An accident. I had trouble piecing the puzzle together.

I am not sure if my calm was drug-induced or if I was in shock, but I did not feel anxious or scared. Both my legs were raised in plaster; my left hand was in an awkward position, held out to the side; and my face felt like it had material all over it, which turned out to be scabs. Several drips above the bed flowed into a needle in my arm.

"Tom, can you hear me?" It was Barry Dinner, our family doctor. I nodded. "Tom, I have some bad news for you, Risto died in the car crash."

How quickly life can change, how fragile it is, how fleeting. What seemed like a few moments were a few days, and what seemed like an eternity were fleeting moments. I was but a tiny cork floating in a tempestuous sea.

As I slipped between a wakeful life of drugs, drips and ablutions, a world of unreal images and a detachment that seemed to beckon to my spirit to give in, I met my Soul for the first time.

In all space and time the place we exist in is not material. I found myself floating in a vacuum. I was naked and detached, an onlooker watching the proceedings. I was not afraid; rather this all seemed strangely familiar. I was aware of other bodies around me. We were all suspended, as if in fluid, we were all naked and waiting for some decision.

I became aware of beings around me, and understood they were discussing me. All of this was familiar and neither intimidating nor foreign. I felt that I had been here before.

A clear question was put to me. "What do you want to do?"

A choice. My choice. I would not be judged for my answer. I was aware of a feeling of great love and compassion. Support. "What do you want to do?"

My answer was clear. "I will return to my home. I have many experiences that I still want to go through, but most importantly I must go to my physical place in the universe to make a contribution."

"Go then, and make your contribution."

I was gasping for air. Panic all around me, people scooting around, concerned. "Make your contribution." I felt familiar warmth in my bed and it was not pleasant, I had peed. As I lay there staring at the ceiling I knew I was back.

"He may walk again if he is lucky, but he will never run. Best you buy him a bike or maybe a canoe, or even encourage him to swim, but his running days are over. I am sorry."

Brian Noll was a great orthopaedic surgeon, one of the best in the country. But he did not understand me. From that day I found a defiance that sometimes scares me.

"Tom you are really, really stubborn," a physiotherapist once told me.

"Dennis, I am single-minded, there is a difference, you know."

Time is a great healer. It was more than my body that needed to bask in its warm passage and passing. It was my mind and my Soul that needed this precious time too. I did eventually heal and I found my strength. Before long I was even thinking of going for a run. But that would be a long way off. I still had a few operations to go under Noll's knife and I had to lose the crutches. But I craved the sweat of a hard workout. How important are our simple pleasures.

It took me a full year to find the courage to find out about Risto's remains. I was in denial and this step was very painful for me. He had been cremated and his ashes placed in a memorial wall in the Braamfontein Cemetery. I went to find his memorial plaque. After some searching, it was there, in solid granite:

"Silvennoinen Risto Olavi"
06.09.56 — 25.12.89
Dearly loved and sadly missed. Rest in peace.

And then in Finnish — *Muistoa Kunnioittaen Omaiset.*

Risto's mother once drew me aside and promised to one day translate, but I am not sure it will ever happen. For me, certain things are best left alone; the meaning may be revealed in another lifetime.

The plane trees are huge and tranquil. Cemeteries seem to have a timeless, spiritual quality that slows us all down to remember and reflect.

I read the plaque for the tenth time, buried my face in my hands, and for the first time in a long time, I began to sob. I wonder if Risto will ever forgive me?

* * *

As waves relentlessly crash on the beach, so does time in our lives. Sally, the widow, returned to Umtata after the funeral to bring up her four-month-old son — Joshua.

She tried to carry on a normal life, but a young vivacious widow in a small town does face challenges. How to "replace" a friend and lover such as her darling Risto? In a small town there is a consummate lack of suitable suitors. Still, the town was not completely bereft of talent. Headly came calling.

Headly was all boisterous puppy-dog. Full of boundless energy, and full of himself. Although by no means short of money, he was very short on the finer points of gentleness and humility. Before long, to my dismay, Headly and Sally were married.

Most of life around Sally, Headly and Joshua became blurred by time and the humdrum of ordinary life — Christmas, Easter, birthdays, a tooth falling out. At some point in the great ongoing tedium, Sally had another son,

Travis. Of course there was family celebration around this event, but Headly was fast isolating his family from the rest of us. To this day he remains an enigma, difficult to understand.

Autumn 1999. Easter time. A change of seasons. Had I been paying more attention I would have heard the distant rumble of a tragedy.

Excitement. With a bit of bartering, scavenging and some plain old recklessness, the Cottrell family planned a two-week holiday in England. The real excuse was the running of the London Marathon, but it was the first time since our Seychelles honeymoon some twenty years earlier that Kay and I were going overseas.

We were due to leave just before Easter, but not before Grand Aunt Sal was to pay us a very welcome visit. Sal arrived with the accustomed fanfare, looking as gorgeous as ever. Imperiously, she marched into my domain with her children in tow. Vivacious, no doubt, but her eyes were dark and tired. And although she sported her sun-bed all-over tan, she had started to develop the ankles of a tired washerwoman and her waistline was beginning to look a bit frumpy.

Headly had gone on a fishing trip with his plumber and building mates from Umtata. A merciful thing. We never did like each other and I didn't want the expectant excitement of London fouled up by Headly's incessant bragging about his racehorses and his wealth.

Joshua was now about ten and his baby brother about four. It was joyous and my daughters were beside themselves with excitement. We would have a few fun-filled days of family mayhem before we departed.

On her arrival Sally imperiously announced, "I'm not feeling that great. Maybe it's a bout of flu coming on."

Both Kay and I unsympathetically held her at arm's length

and marched her off to the spare bedroom. More like the isolation ward. We had trained hard and were going to run the London Marathon, there was no way we were going to expose ourselves to Sally's germs.

With the approaching holiday, Sally's condition was not getting any better. She stayed in bed and our family entertained the boys. One morning she woke us at 4:00 am. She held up her nightie, exposing a swollen tummy. She was in agony and begged to be taken to the emergency ward, NOW!

It is difficult to give detail of the next few days, save to say they passed by in a fog. Our emotions were pounded on the exposed rocks like small tugboats in a hurricane.

One moment we were admitting Sally to the hospital and the next, frantic calls were being made to Betty and Basil to tell them to get to the hospital before it was too late. In a haze, calls were made to Headly, on a remote island off Mozambique. The waves crashed down and the tide ran in and we were swept into the boiling water. In one instant Sally was being chided by a young intern for wasting their time with "mild pain". The next day she was in the Intensive Care Unit fighting for her life.

Sally was diagnosed with Toxic Shock Syndrome, a bacterial infection often associated with the use of tampons and contraceptive devices in women.

The tide was running out. A learned and calm doctor sat down with the family and tried to explain why Sally was on every known life-support system and was likely never to respond again: "Many people experience a two- to three-day period of mild symptoms before they develop the disease. These may include low-grade fever, muscle aches, chills, and a feeling of general ill health."

We clung to each other as passengers had done on the tilting decks of the Titanic. Able to see disaster before us, but unable to either comprehend or acknowledge the inevitable. The doctor went on: "Symptoms develop suddenly, and the disease can be fatal. It affects the organ systems in the body, the skin, lungs, liver, kidneys, blood and pancreas."

"When one major bodily system shuts down," he explained, "there is a fifty percent chance that we can save the patient." He drew breath, watching us carefully. "When two major systems shut down there is an eighty percent chance that we may lose the patient." The boat was tilting dangerously.

"To put this into perspective, four of Sally's major organ systems have shut down. I am sorry, but we are going to lose her."

Our minds reeling, our emotions crashing, thousands of unanswered questions — we clung to each other. So confusing, out of control. The iceberg had struck, the boat was sinking.

The morning we were due to leave for London, I sat in the garden holding Kay's hand. Neither of us had slept the night before. The autumn sun was warm and the daylight was a welcome relief.

"Kay, it's your call. The plane leaves tonight, but if you decide to stay, we as a family will understand and we will support you." Sally was dying.

With the sagely advice of our close friends, Wendy and Sue, the decision was finally, agonisingly made. We were going to London. The plane was due to leave at 8:00 pm. We made our way to the hospital for the last time.

In slow motion, in a timeless void of pain and sadness, we walked down the long sterile corridors to the ICU. There may have been a thousand people scurrying around, or the corridors could have been empty. It was the four of us: Kay, Sally's sister; Megan and Bronwyn, her nieces; and me, more than just a brother-in-law. I, who carried the guilt of Risto's death. I felt there were so many questions I had to answer in Joshua's mind. As a family we said goodbye to Sally.

The ride to the airport that evening was a silent one.

CHAPTER 4

Living through the Revolution

—oOo—

I was drunk, the guy I was embracing was drunk, and for one moment in time we both knew that South Africa would be a great place to bring up our children. He, a black tradesman from Soweto; I, a white accountant from Greenside, at an impromptu street party in the late winter of 1995.

It broke out minutes after the final whistle went and Francois Pienaar held the Webb Ellis Trophy aloft as South Africa became the World Rugby Champions. The evening was cold, but the fires gave the throbbing mass a gathering point of friendship. The warmth of people dancing and shouting and sharing. A roller-coaster ride. In a few short years, we had come from pariah state and outcast country, to a Rainbow Nation.

I remember so clearly the day that the South African

President, FW de Klerk, made the dramatic announcement. It was in February 1990. I was in hospital, recovering from my car accident. The African National Congress (ANC) will be unbanned, so will the Communist Party. Nelson Mandela will be released from prison.

How could one not feel moved? We were living through history's most miraculous revolution. This was a new nation. How funny it all seems now, more than a decade on, that people stockpiled tinned food and water as South Africa felt its way forward from a racially divided past.

On voting day — April 27, 1994 — I stood for hours in a queue, absorbing an atmosphere never experienced before. People came and made their mark on our first legitimate democracy. This election opened the batting and we intended a big score. Each of us voted for our hopes rather than our fears.

When Nelson Mandela was inaugurated as president, it underscored what a great team we had. More than ten years on, and the "Madiba Magic" seems to have lost some of its potency. But it would be exhausting, if not impossible to live at such a pace. The party is over, the honeymoon done. Now we have to get down to making the miracle work.

Here I am, a pale male in the place of my birth. Living through a revolution was never going to be easy, yet every person I have ever canvassed does not want the old country back. I look back, not only on the last ten years, but on all of my fifty. I am glad to be here, I feel gratitude to have travelled this path. I am an African.

I remain confused. I see areas of the country falling into disrepair. Health services and hospitals, education and crime. Depression and pessimism.

But then I look around again, and I see vibrancy and vigour. Recently in a Soweto shebeen I witnessed the warmest and friendliest people in all of Africa. I see a country flexing its muscles, finding its self-confidence.

There is friendliness and openness with all the people I encounter, and there is honesty too. We have learned to shake hands; we have learned the social graces of differing cultures. I have lived through this revolution and I am glad.

I knew there was a miracle taking place when I watched the televised Truth and Reconciliation Commission (TRC) hearings. It was a time South Africa took to listen to its soul. A time when we could embrace each other and ask for forgiveness. It would take a man of great spiritual resources to lead such a process, and South Africa is blessed with such a courageous spirit in Desmond Tutu.

No matter how I try to justify it, planting a bomb in a restaurant is the lowest form of cowardice. A callous and cynical action. So when a bomb ripped through Magoo's Bar in Durban in 1986, killing three people and wounding seventy-three others, I was angry. Robert McBride had planted the bomb. At the time he was a unit commander in the ANC's special operations unit. He received three death sentences for the bombing, but was given a reprieve when the ANC demanded an end to political executions, as a precondition to negotiations with the National Party.

My mind was closed when I watched the McBride hearings. How could such a callous attack be carried out? And yet, when I saw this man asking for forgiveness from the victims and their relatives, I had a deep sense of my own need to forgive and ask for forgiveness.

What was in the mind of McBride at the time of the hearings? What was in his heart? Who can really tell? But it was the humaneness in the process that stuck with me. Whether it was carefully stage-managed or a genuine outpouring of the human spirit, I cannot be sure. But I was touched deeply, in my own small way.

It is true that I benefited from a good government education, enjoyed so many privileges ahead of my black countrymen. I did not protest. I did not show much defiance at a system that was so unjust, but which benefited me. Yet I watched the drama played out in the McBride hearings, and I felt a sense of forgiveness and ease.

I am not sure how to carry this forgiveness forward in a way that is meaningful to myself or those I have unconsciously hurt. I am not even sure of the content or the substance of my guilt, but I do know that by emotionally letting Robert McBride go, I am a little more free.

Could Palestinians and Jewish families ever find such forgiveness? Could they ever let go? Could we let go of the Holocaust? What of the Bosnians and Serbs, the Greeks and the Turks? Can we grasp the end of our special Rainbow and give it to the rest of the world? I am no political analyst; just one player in a game with over forty million people on the team. Living through history's most peaceful revolution.

Finding a sense of belonging has been part of my own South African experience. Figuring others and myself out on this level has transformed my spirit. There is a strong emotional intelligence about Africa. It is a place of many contrasts with its rhythms and its beat, its light and its shadows. But it has always had a warm and generous heart.

I can see this in the attitudes of my children. They will carry this revolution to a logical conclusion. For me it is enough that I embrace Robert McBride and forgive him, and that I am sorry for not joining the struggle. Herein lies my private liberation struggle.

* * *

The bullets ripped into the trees above me as I lay pressing my face into the dust. I never knew that fear had such a timelessness about it. I had been married for only a few months, had just started a new job. When I got back from my stint on "the border" I was to start a part-time degree at Wits University. My whole life lay ahead, full of promise.

Another thing I found out about fear that day is that it relaxes both bladder and bowel.

In the mid to late seventies South Africa pushed the limits of its war-mongering into Angola. Such insatiable stupidity required enormous resources in men, machines and money. None of us could escape. All males out of school had to join the army or face imprisonment.

Over the Christmas holidays of 1977/1978 I found myself in northern Namibia. I was regimental paymaster, and for this weighty and responsible job I was promoted to Corporal. The job was great once you got used to the idea of living in a tent with four other guys, one of whom was criminally insane.

I had to pay the troops once a month at appointed camps and sites in the bush. My assistant was as brainless as they come, a young farmer from Koster who operated the Browning mounted on the back of the Jeep. He was there to see that the SWAPO insurgents did not steal the army guy's money.

The job had great perks. I could use the Jeep outside of my normal paymaster duties, and once everyone had been paid, my job was done. I found that I had about twenty days off in the month. Hey, great stuff. I had time to relax and catch up on my reading. I was based at Grootfontein and the military precincts boasted a swimming pool and a library. My army stint on the border was going to be fun, even if it was at the taxpayers' expense.

The South African army was strict about keeping soldiers out of the civilian areas of Grootfontein. One could only go into the town on business, and you were not allowed to be there for long. The Military Police set up barricades across the main road into the town.

One of the main attractions of Grootfontein was Pappa's, a

general dealer owned by a lively Greek called Nick. At Pappa's one could buy the biggest hamburgers in all of Christendom. They were the tastiest and juiciest any soldier could lay his hands on. Add to that a packet of *slap* chips, alongside an ice-cold Coke, and military life could become almost civilised.

My relationship with the Military Police was good. And why not? I was their paymaster. For me to make regular visits to Pappa's was easy. "Hey Corporal Payman, when are we getting paid?" the MPs would call out as they waved me through the booms. The deal was, and there was always a deal, that I should buy the guards hamburgers and Cokes.

And so my army life settled down into a steady routine of visits to the Olympic-size swimming pool, the library and Pappa's.

One or two other people seemed to have as much time on their hands as I. Pretty soon I started talking to an older guy at the pool. Keith was guarded on his opinions of the army but was expansive on almost every other subject under the sun. When I suggested that we pop into town for a burger and Coke, he was delighted.

On our return, Keith asked me to drop him off at the main admin building where most of the officers were housed. By his bearing and confidence I knew something was different and as far as I was concerned, wrong. Keith invited me to follow him as he strode confidently into a major's office.

"Morning Brigadier," said the major as he stood up. "Oh, shit," I thought.

"It seems as if my friend, the Corporal, is under-utilised. Do you think you can use him, Major?"

"Oh, shit," I thought. My mate Keith was a high-ranking officer in the operational area taking a few days break before he was shipped back home to South Africa.

I was given a crash course in recovery work. Before I knew

it I was in charge of an overgrown tow-truck with six demented and enthusiastic guys that I had nothing in common with. I was not relieved of my paymaster job, and now I was running this tow-truck business for the army, recovering civilian cars stuck in the sand and fetching the odd army truck that had run out of petrol miles from nowhere.

The call came early one morning just after the regimental Christmas party. One of our armoured vehicles had driven over a landmine and there were casualties. Our truck was on duty and it was our job to bring the vehicle back to Grootfontein for repairs or scrapping.

The army has a set procedure: evacuate the injured, sweep the area for other mines, and guard the vehicle until the recovery unit arrives. There should be a fairly safe passage in and out.

We spotted the camouflaged wreck in the bush. We had driven for over eight hours and were keen to hook-up and go home. It all seemed fairly standard and routine, and I told one of the guys, "Go into the vehicle and release the handbrake."

Then came the loud explosion as a mine blew into his body. Suddenly, guns were going off nearby. One of our recovery guys screamed and doubled over as a bullet tore into his flesh. It felt like an hour, but it must have taken only a few seconds. Ambush.

I was poorly equipped for this. Being a bank clerk and a part-time student, I was not a big army fellow. I hated guns and tried every trick in the book to get out of visits to the shooting range. Dirk, a fearless Afrikaner mechanic from Alberton, was animated. He jumped into our tow-truck's turret and cocked the Browning. He let loose with a volley of shots that was so loud, it must have wakened the gatekeepers of Hell.

The return fire tore into Dirk and I watched in dazed amazement as his head exploded like a watermelon spewing red and white matter.

"Oh, God — I am going to die here," I thought.

I never realised it, but a magazine of automatic fire does not go on and on like in the movies. It takes only a few seconds. In the next few seconds it went quiet. The shooting had stopped.

There was a movement and a groan close to me. I crawled over to the noise and found one of our guys, hurt, but alive. I held him in my arms, I felt that I was there, but not there. I was an observer and a participant all at once.

"Ah fuck, it hurts," said the guy in Afrikaans.

I am not sure how long I sat holding him; he seemed to be sleeping. Time in that place seemed to take on dimensions that I could not understand.

"Promise me, Corporal Pay, that if I die, you will tell my wife and kids that I loved them."

"Hey man, no one is going to die. We will go home, we will build empires and we will love our families. Stay with it now Sarel, help will come."

When I tried to deal with this in my own way back home, I felt a certain detachment from life that was going on around me. I kept my promise to Sarel and went to see his wife and children. I explained to them how their father died a great hero fighting "terrorists" in South West Africa. No matter what I said, no matter what I did, I was left with an overwhelming sense of guilt that I had survived this ordeal while six other men had died.

For more than a year afterwards, I would catch the bus home from work. Not the normal one that took me home, but the one that stopped in Rosebank. Every Thursday I would buy a bunch of flowers and a bottle of wine, and walk home to Kay. This was the walk of life.

A few months later a parcel was delivered to my door. It was a medal from Pretoria together with a certificate for framing. An orange ribbon with blue stripes. The medal had an aloe in the centre. I sat in my study in silence and stared at the certificate. I felt empty and numb. I felt nothing.

A poem of WB Yeats came to mind as I held the certificate. I reached for a felt-tipped pen and wrote over the certificate the words of the great poet ...

Turning and turning in the widening gyre
The falcon cannot hear the falconer;
Things fall apart; the centre cannot hold;
Mere anarchy is loosed upon the world,
The blood-dimmed tide is loosed, and everywhere
The ceremony of innocence is drowned;
The best lack all conviction, while the worst
Are full of passionate intensity.

In some way Corporal Pay died in that place too. I felt, for the sake of my own sanity, that somehow I had to free myself from the guilt, also the feeling of ... well, of nothing. In a small private ritual I set that certificate alight and watched it burn to ashes. I gathered these up and placed them in a matchbox and then buried them. Years on I sometimes hear the subtle but distinct cry in the night of my dying comrades.

Ashes to ashes, dust to dust — there is still a weak and faint tremble in a heartbeat, still an echo in a melody long forgotten. Even a split-second's hesitancy in a handshake or a flicker in the eye — it is there in the shadows. Corporal Pay whispers, "I'll always be with you."

* * *

No one really watched Gert Thys run into the Olympic Stadium in Atlanta in 1996. He was well out of the placings, running a disappointing marathon. The camera was on him though, and a few noticed that he left the track and spoke briefly to Josiah Thugwane, now huddled against the cool air after his historic win. The camera caught the two speaking, Josiah nodded and smiled, Gert gave a thumbs up and finished the race.

Afterwards someone asked Gert what he said to Thugwane. "I saw him with the flag, so I knew he was in the placings. I asked him what colour medal he won. Josie smiled and simply said 'yellow'. I really respect that, man."

Josiah was the very last runner expected to take gold. He made the squad only because he had won the South African Marathon Championships. He was not there because of his times, there were faster contenders, but the sponsors insisted that the winner be included in the squad.

The early parts of the Atlanta marathon saw a fairly good showing by the South African team. The tactic was simple enough, keep Gert Thys covered, protect him, and when the time came, he would move into contention and take the gold. As the race wore on, and as wills began to wilt in the heat and humidity, it was Josiah who took up the challenge and moved into the front.

The diminutive runner bravely stayed in the hunt for a medal. At thirty-eight kilometres, with only four to go, there were three runners in contention for the medal. Kenya's Erick Wainaina, looking every bit a honed and fluid running machine; Lee Bong-ju from Korea; and Josiah. This was the biggest race of his life; he went deep into himself to find sagely advice. Jacques Malan, his coach, teacher and mentor was a simple but clear guide, "Run this race like you run any other race at home. It is no different."

With only twenty metres to go, it looked as though the Korean would surely overtake the tiny man in green and gold. But the ribbon and the gold belonged to Josiah. His win by three seconds is the closest in Olympian Marathon history.

In South Africa, the excitement was felt throughout the nation. In the small town of Bethal, at the Koornfontein Mine, grown men were crying, women ululating, and children running around as if there was no tomorrow. Once more, once again, the fledgling nation had found something to reaffirm our greatness: a small man with a big heart.

Josiah carried with him in that race the mark of a hijacker's bullet on his chin. Josiah made extra money as a driver, delivering beer to rural shebeens in his bakkie. The hijacker stopped him, climbed into the passenger seat and told him to drive. He decided to kill Josiah, who escaped death by a hair's breadth when he jumped out of the moving vehicle.

"I was banged about a bit and I broke my front tooth." He explains. "But the worst part was that the fall injured me for running. I thought my chances of going to America were zero. I took a chance and went to Albuquerque to train with the squad in May. I was lucky and relieved because I came right."

The former cattle herder who captured gold has had a dramatic life since his win in Atlanta. He has been shot at, victimised. He once had a monkey's head placed at his front door. He has also been troubled by indifferent performances, injury and personal grief.

Josiah's victory was not the end of an Olympic dream. For the young man it was the start of a new race, a different marathon. His is a story of triumph over the odds in the journey of life. One of the first things that Josiah did under the continuing tutelage of Jacques, was to learn to read and write. It was also important for him to express himself in the media, so he learned to speak English.

When Josiah went to Sydney in 2000, he was only the third

man ever in Olympic history to defend the marathon title. Sadly, Jacques Malan was not at his side, for the teacher, mentor and coach had passed on. Cancer. Many wonder if the death of such a man as Jacques had an effect on Josiah. Josiah has the last word; he looks wistfully out of a window, "One of the most important things that I learned from Malan," he explains in English, "was how to keep my spirit strong. I will always need a strong spirit to win."

* * *

Standing at the ticket counter at the airport one evening I heard an exchange behind me.

"Hi Megan, I'm surprised to see you here."

The voice of a man in his early twenties, educated. Definitely private school. Johannesburg northern suburbs. The accent was St Johns or maybe St Stithians.

"Hi Vun, I'm going back early. I have a lot of work to catch up and besides, I'm tired of lying around my parent's house like a toad. Dad, meet Vundla, he's in my psychology class. Vundla, this is my dad."

As I turned around I faced a tall, well-built young man. Of course he was black, but what struck me was his easy, comfortable manner. He stuck out his hand and we shook warmly.

"Hi, Mr Cottrell, pleased to meet you at last. Megan has told me a lot about you."

Megan and Vun stand arm-in-arm, obviously comfortable in each other's presence. We smile and chat about Rhodes; about the rigours of living in Johannesburg. Megan and Vun were pleased to get seats on the plane next to each other and Vun was happy to give Megan a lift from the airport once they landed.

I may be forgiven for finding this incident at the airport worthy of a mention. It is true that the meeting was as normal and as natural as any, and could have taken place anywhere in the world — except for one small detail: such an event could never have happened eleven years ago in the same airport, and that is the miracle.

A revolution takes twenty-five years to work its way through the system. The mindsets of those who started the revolution are different from those who will finish it. For my children, apartheid is just an absurd concept dreamed up by us baby-boomers. For them, Mandela has always been free.

Each man lives life according to the inner beat of body and soul. We are placed here, in societies with certain religious or political convictions, born a certain race. I am here, in this place, a white man, born in this African country. I am first and foremost a human being, and I seek to bind myself with all, because of my humanity, not because of my nationality.

I have been a companion traveller on this path and I must acknowledge all those around me. I look at my fellows in South Africa. I see my daughter deeply engrossed in conversation with Vundla. They are sitting at a table in a coffee shop, oblivious of my presence. Their manner is easy as Megan lightly touches his hand and laughs.

My children will finish the South African revolution and I am glad.

CHAPTER 5

Africa

The eco-balance of all things and the sacredness of family

———o0o———

He knelt on the soft earth. His eyes, accustomed to the dark, darted from side to side. He picked up a small pinch of dung and held it to his nose. Fresh. He was closing in on his quarry.

Inyathi, the Great Buffalo, was a respected Zulu *isangoma*. He was a proud man, revered in his community and consulted often on matters of importance by those who lived in the shadow of the Great Mountain, Inchanga. The ancestors had sent him on a strange mission, one not even he, with the wisdom of the ages, could easily understand. Dressed in traditional skins, Inyathi blended into the landscape. Here in veld and bush, on the great planes and in the damp forests, he was at home. He looked skywards and noted the angle of the pointers to the Southern Cross. Soon dawn would break. Inyathi sighed and moved on.

This *isangoma* spent many years on the mountain slopes learning about the fragile balance of nature. The Great Buffalo understood how Oxpecker lived off the great herds. He knew that rich soil produced succulent feed. He lived with Lion and understood how she hunted; her need to feed the pride. The Great Buffalo knew many of the secrets of Africa.

We in the universe are all One Body. Each of us is connected. The good, the evil, and all beings in-between. And what of the evil? Does the tree withhold its fruit from the unworthy? iNkosi yezulu, the Lord-of-the-Sky, was driving Inyathi on. The source of both good and evil, iNkosi yezulu was herding his son into the dawn, and Inyathi did not know why.

He took a small drink at the stream. The water sweet and cool on his lips.

Even the fish and other creatures that live in this water understand the interconnectedness of the Universe. If the source of this river is bad, the water is bad. If all that flows from the highest mountain is tainted, then those who depend on its quenching shall surely die.

"Fathers," Inyathi would tell those at the village, "Jealously guard the source of the river. All life, all goodness flows from this point. The source is the most important part of the river, it dictates what happens downstream."

"Do not think that it is only the great herds on plains and in forests that are important. The ants that carry away what is left of the carcass, those that eat the dung of the great ones, they are great too. For it is the workers of nature that hold its fabric together.

"This is true of each man and woman in the village too. For each life is connected to and dependent on the next. If one should die, as we all must at some time, the fabric of the society changes. We do not know whether it will change for better or for worse, but it will change.

Inyathi moved easily now. He thought of the nature and life of each man. A man has many parts. A man's thoughts are not separate from his body, and his body is surely not separate from his spirit.

Can a man's wisdom be greater than that of his ancestors? Inyathi thought about his dead mother, gregarious and loud. He also thought of his grandmother, a great spirit who had guarded his own spirit. She would come to him often and chide him for his earthly excesses. He could see her now, standing like a guardian before him, silent, unsmiling. Loving him.

Inyathi's family was large and boisterous. He felt part of it and was pleased to play an important role in its affairs. There was always deep discussion before any decision. Each member had a turn to express their hopes and fears. If the decision was big, Inyathi would take the problem and lay it before his ancestors and patiently wait for an answer.

Family was a great source of his strength and comfort. The Great Buffalo loved his family and would spend much of his time teaching them the ways of the people, how to be confident. If the next generation is to carry forward the torch of the Great Buffalo, they must know who they are, so they can carry the fire with dignity and pride. Inyathi was the source of his family's river.

Dawn had broken. First light made soft shadows and nature's stirrings gave the darkness an edge. Inyathi sighed, the search was over for a while, he must blend into the day ...

* * *

I rolled over and stared at the ceiling. I had been having disturbing dreams lately. The mists of the dreams retracted faster than my mind could get to them. I lay there, trying to catch the dream as it disappeared into some unreachable recess. It was something strange. There was someone chasing me, looking for me. I just couldn't make out who.

I lay in the bath, still staring at the ceiling.

"So, Tom, how is your training going?"

"Not bad at all, Terry. I'm carrying a bit too much weight, but I've put in some long-distance runs, I should be ready."

"It's only two weeks away to your first marathon. How do you feel?"

"Difficult to say really, I know that I will be running throughout the year, so I don't focus on any one particular race. I will do steady, consistent training throughout the year. That way you can manage such a long, drawn out programme. It all seems a bit distant and unreal, but I think that once I have made the first journey to East London and arrive at the start, I'll be okay."

"Are you worried about injury, Tom?"

"Always a worry. But I believe in a sane approach, especially on race day. I always think of my training run on the Tuesday after the race. Run in such a way that you can make the recovery, and run the following Tuesday. Do that, Terry, and you will cut your injuries down to almost nothing."

"What, may I ask, do you do on Mondays?"

"Mondays are always rest days, no matter what. You need to allow your body to recover, and I do nothing. It doesn't seem that big a deal when you are running the shorter distances, but believe me, when you run further than twenty kilometres on a Sunday, you need the rest. Tuesdays is a recovery run. On Wednesdays I swim."

"You swim?"

"A way to give variety to training. It builds good upper body strength, and takes the pressure off my legs, especially where my ankle broke. Thursdays I use for a fairly hard and long run, Fridays I run with my friends. We meet at Zoo Lake and go for a feisty, but talkative jog. Saturday it's back into the pool. I do about 1600 metres and then a long run on Sunday."

"How long is your run on Sunday?"

"It depends, between twenty and thirty-seven kilometres. I use the hard-easy principle. I have a hard week of training, followed by an easier week. That way I am able to slowly but surely strengthen my body. Like stretching an elastic band. If you do it too suddenly it will break. Stretch it out slowly, and then relax it, stretch it out slowly, just a little further, and relax, and the band won't break, but you will stretch it a lot further."

"This is all very interesting Tom, now ..."

I put up my hand, we are running out of time, already my bathwater has run out and the phone is ringing in the next room.

I stand in the middle of the room, dripping. "Hello, Tom speaking ..." It is Jennifer Jones, a psychologist confirming my appointment later that day.

Kay is surprised when I tell her over dinner one evening that I am seeing a shrink. Gently the music plays in the background. Candles flicker, I try to put a sensible perspective on it, but even in these safe surroundings, it is difficult to explain my emotions beyond an uncomfortable feeling.

I want to make my ordinary life special. I am reaching an important milestone and I want so much more. Oh yes, I know about middle-age breakdowns, and I don't want to go down that road. I have no desire for a Ferrari and I don't want my tongue pierced. While I would like to try my hand at a young blonde affair, Kay strongly cautions me against this, and warns me that this activity is fraught with danger.

In all seriousness I feel so irrelevant. My life has run away from me, and I have so little to show for it. That is why I am paying Jenny a visit.

* * *

As I lay on the psychologist's couch, hugging a pillow, I tried to get in touch with my feelings.

It was odd, the closest I had ever been to a psychologist was a view of a consulting room in the movies. This was just like the movies, and I felt that I was part of a script. This was reality though, the clock ticked on the wall and the woman before me sat with detached professionalism, prodding here and there, hoping to kick over some rock and disturb the psyche's ants.

As a runner I recognise the need for outside medical help when I have an injury. Injuries are part of a runner's life, particularly in the early stages. It takes a certain knowing and experience to understand when you can run through an injury or when you need to visit the physiotherapist. The logic of my visit to the shrink was established along just such lines. I had sustained a psychological injury, it was more than just a niggle.

On the couch I wrestled with an emotion no word could describe, yet this woman was pressing me to put words to it. Not anger, yet in part it was. Neither was it frustration, although that was why I was here. I grappled with it, but nothing came. There was an emptiness. That was just the point. An empty void.

Life comprises many catalysts that spur people to do things. It was my eldest daughter's behaviour when I dropped her off at university that saw me lying here now. I was excited for Megan, now at Rhodes University, going into her second year of a psychology degree. She wanted to move out of home and experience a residential university. For Kay and me there were no boundaries to our joy when, against Megan's own odds, she was accepted at Rhodes.

Megan was a special child right from her early schooling. We detected subtle and yet profound learning difficulties. We budgeted for ongoing occupational therapy throughout her school career. Megan was a determined child who showed great courage. It was a family achievement to get to the day Megan went to Rhodes.

But as I drove home I was seething inside because of the off-handed way she had said goodbye. She was busy on her cell phone and I was impatient to leave and get to Cradock before dark. The farewells were a fractious combination of ill temper, petulance, and stupidity. By the time I got home, I was feeling desolate and knew I needed to see someone.

I tried to come to grips with the real problem. I had been a good family man. I did play my part. Right from an early age I valued and envied the family unit. I knew that it was an important aspect of human growth. I set about the task of building a family almost from my high school days, when I set about courting Kay, my bride.

Our table was always a place of discussion, a place to catch up on the news of the day. My garden was an obstacle course, and beyond the balls, the bikes and the jungle gym were the shadows. There, in those mystical shadows, lived the fairies, gnomes and elves. We would hunt them in the moonlight. It was a place where the Tooth Fairy lived, the Easter Bunny visited.

What of Kay? I look at her after almost thirty years of marriage. She is not the beauty she was. As with me, there are signs of ageing. Just like me she is sagging here, greying there, and she, too, bears battle scars. She has been my companion, my fellow traveller, for more than half of my life. Over this time I have learned a deeper meaning of the word "love".

How do I love thee?
Let me count the ways.
I love thee to the depth and breadth and height
My soul can reach, when feeling out of sight
For the ends of Being and ideal Grace.
I love thee to the level of everyday's
Most quiet need, by sun and candle-light.
I love thee freely, as men strive for Right;
I love thee purely, as they turn from Praise.
I love thee with a passion put to use
In my old griefs, and with my childhood's faith.
I love thee with a love I seemed to lose
With my lost saints,
I love thee with the breath,
Smiles, tears, of all my life!
and, if God choose,
I shall but love thee better after death.
(Elizabeth Barrett Browning)

Into my life came three women who changed everything. They brought with them an ideal grace. First came Kay, and then two daughters, Megan and Bronwyn. Each came to me as a unique individual. This, then, was my family, a unit that would provide hope, safety and strength. It is a privilege to be a member of such a loving, caring unit. My family is the most important part of my make-up and personality.

Wise men I revere speak of family. Cicero, two thousand years ago, said: "The home is the empire, there is no peace more delightful than one's own fireplace". Samuel Johnson agreed: "To be happy at home is the ultimate result of all ambition."

I understood all of this, lived such a life. So why was I lying on this couch, in this room, feeling so empty? My family was growing up and finding their own way in the world. Time to move on. This did not come to me as a bolt from the blue, but rather as a creeping realisation. My job of growing and nurturing a young family was done.

I left the psychologist's room and sat in my car a bit dazed. The shift in life's emphasis was still new. I had told Jenny my life's story. Everything. Well nearly everything. But there were these strange dreams I had been having. Someone, some strange force was hunting me, tracking me. The recurring dream of someone looking for me. I drove off wondering why I did not tell her that ...

* * *

"So tell me Tom, who is your greatest hero, living or dead ..."

Terry loves to open the conversation, and I think he is getting even better at his job.

"Well Terry — living has to be Kay."

"Naa," says Terry. "You're just saying that to earn some brownie points, aren't you?"

"No, Terry. It's true. Once, Kay was running the Comrades when early on in the race she tripped on a cat's-eye in the road and fell. She grazed her hands, her knee and her chin. Yet she didn't give in. She got up and carried on running. She fell a second time and got up and ran to finish.

"I met her at the end of the race when she came in an hour later than expected. I was concerned. Her vest was covered in blood, her knees were a mess and her hands were bleeding. That shows guts. Lesser mortals would have thrown in the towel. Kay is a great hero to me, not only because of that incident, but also for many other things.

"She is deaf. You wouldn't think so, but it's true. She has only twenty percent hearing but she is a teacher in a primary school. That is a true hero. One who overcomes adversity. If a person is faced with great obstacles, there is definitely 'hero' potential in that life."

"And your greatest dead hero?"

"Either Beethoven or Gandhi.

"Beethoven's Ninth Symphony is the most majestic piece I have ever heard: *The Ode to Joy*. When Beethoven wrote this symphony he was almost completely deaf. He sawed the legs off a piano and rested the whole thing on the floor. Between banging on the floor and writing, he finished this masterpiece. Nothing was going to stand in the way of greatness.

"Beethoven insisted that he conduct the concert's premiere, but the organisers were really, really worried. He was known for his foul temper, and what Mr Beethoven wanted — Beethoven got. How could a deaf conductor lead an orchestra? The organisers had a plan. They placed a second conductor in the wings, where the orchestra could see him, but Beethoven could not.

"The curtain rose and the Ninth played to a capacity crowd, finishing on a majestic note. The audience had never heard such music and were ecstatic. There was wild and thunderous applause, and there stood the great composer, unhearing and totally unaware of the audience's appreciation.

"The lead violinist walked up to the great man — 'Maestro' he gently turned him around to face the appreciative audience. I wish I had been there, for I believe that must have been one of music history's greatest moments. A moment of sublime grace and courage. Kay represents both the grace and the courage of the Maestro. Her deafness has never stopped her from being the artist she is.

"And Gandhi, here was a man who wore a loincloth, who was not head of a government, had no army, and embraced all faiths. This was a man who brought England to its knees. He was a really special person, with faith and humanity worthy of admiration.

"Gandhi also had great wisdom when it came to families and homes. There is a statue of him that stands in a small garden in Washington. A quotation is inscribed on a plaque — 'I do not want my house to be walled on all sides and my windows to be stuffed. I want the cultures of all the lands to be blown about my house as freely as possible. But I refuse to be blown off my feet by any. I refuse to live in other people's houses as an interloper or a slave.'

"Terry — my water is getting cold now. Can we finish this some other time?"

* * *

Inyathi could sense he was getting close. The Great Buffalo in the shadows was watching. Another Dawn was breaking, his journey was nearly over.

Soon he would return home, but first he had to find someone, someone in the mists, someone nearby ...

"Holy shit! Who are you, what are you doing here?" I woke with a start. There was a black man standing at the foot of my bed. Dressed in skins with a leopard skin headband. He did not move, he locked his arms. His face without expression.

"My name is Inyathi, the Great Buffalo, the Spirits have sent me here to run with you ..."

* * *

By any standards, the Buffalo Marathon field is modest. It is a point-to-point race. Runners must simply drive some forty kilometres out of East London on the Queenstown road, and run back. At some point in the middle of a dark and misty African dawn, a banner is stretched across the road. The start is devoid of any pomp or circumstance, but the runners around me are warm and friendly. No more than seven hundred runners line up on the main Queenstown road this morning. All indications are that we will have perfect running conditions. The cloud cover will ensure that, as long as the rain holds off.

I saw him in the crowd at the start. The throng was getting impatient to begin the race. We held eye contact for a second or two and he nodded. It was this Zulu chap that I had been dreaming of. I looked again. Here he was, the guy in my dreams. The gun went and the race crowd shuffled forward. Small and understated this may be, but I am in awe of the start, and for me the end is a long, long way ahead. The finish line at Buffalo Park is only the beginning. Kay squeezed my hand, "Good luck, have a good run." "Thanks, you too." I shuffle off on my pilgrimage.

The early parts of this marathon pass through the rural districts of the Eastern Cape. It is March, the end of summer, and the villages are set on an emerald carpet. The road snakes its way to East London, through rolling hills and mist. A quiet road. I breathe deeply; the air is sweet. I am alive and I am here, Africa is my home. Today is my birthday. I feel a special sense of occasion. As a special gift Kay is going to hold back and run the whole race with me. I joke with the runners close by that the rule is she has to run three paces behind me, the whole way, and sing my praises. And Terry is here ... doing an interview on the run.

We settle into a good, modest pace. I know there are some hard hills at the end, so I want to hold back something in reserve. Running a marathon is like playing a game of cards. Each card is a unit of energy. The real trick is to be stingy with the cards in your hand, and play them judiciously. If you play your hand right you should have more than half the pack in your hand with five kilometres to go.

A long-distance race allows for silence and introspection. I am getting into an easy and comfortable stride, and the kilometre marker boards are going past at more or less six-minute intervals. I can look forward to five hours of birthday celebration, in the way I had chosen.

Then again, I see this Zulu, now running ahead of me,

sweating profusely and muttering to himself. I draw up to his shoulder. "Hi, how you doing?" He gives me a look that is not friendly. "You are the cause of all of my suffering today. What is it that you have to tell me?"

"Nothing. I have nothing to say to you, and why are you following me around?"

"The Great Spirit told me to find you. I must run with you. Now I am in a hurry and I want to return to my village and my community."

"Well, if you are going to run with me, there are a few rules. Firstly, don't be so rude. My name is Tom, what is yours?"

"Inyathi, the Great Buffalo."

"This is my wife, Kay." Inyathi scowled and nodded. Kay did not respond.

"Where do you come from?"

"I live near Inchanga, in the Valley of a Thousand Hills. Where are we running to?"

"We are running a marathon. To East London."

"How far is it?"

"Forty-two kilometres."

"How far is that?"

Inchanga is a notorious hill on the Comrades Marathon route. I know the terrain like I know the pattern on my running shoes.

"We are going to run from Inchanga to the heart of eThekwini, to Durban."

"But that is a two-day walk."

"Hey, Inyathi — we will be there before teatime today."

Silence.

"By the way, I think you've gone out much too fast. If you are going to run with me, you better get your pacing right — otherwise you are going to blow."

When I started running long-distance races, Professor Tim

Noakes gave a lecture on running the marathon and beyond. There he stood, the guru on the podium, and his message was simple but frightening. "There is no physical reason why a runner should be on their feet after running more than thirty-two kilometres. The geographical halfway mark may well be at twenty-one kilometres, but the real half way starts only after thirty kilometres of running.

"No matter how much you ingest prior to the race, your body can only hold so much and no more. Yes, it is carbohydrates that will carry you to the finish, and you must eat a lot of food rich in carbos, pasta and the like, but physically there is a limit."

"There is more bad news. Taking in carbohydrates on the run can't help that much either. It takes time for the food to be ingested, digested, and then to leave the stomach and to get into the blood stream. It takes longer to do that than it takes to run a marathon."

"So here is the challenge of the marathon. You will all get hypoglycaemia. Your blood sugar levels are going to fall very low and you will still have ten kilometres to run. This is the tantalising part of a marathon. This is why people *have* to do it. Emil Zatopek — the only runner in Olympic history to win three distance events in the same games — once said, 'If you want to run, run a mile; if you want to experience a new life — run a marathon'.

"The final stages of a marathon are run mainly on your own spiritual and mental resources, this is where the soul of the race lies. This, then, is the challenge of the marathon."

I muse about Tim's lecture, wondering also about this belligerent Zulu. I know deep down why he has come to me. We have just run past the halfway mark, but he is not ready for me yet.

"What is Happiness?" Terry puffing away. Nice one, old man, it helps pass the time.

"Well, Terry ..." I pause. I have to look back over my life and think. After fifty years, what makes me happy?

"Well, Terry ..." I stop again. I really need to think. Next to me Kay is talking to another runner and I slip back a step or two, just so that I can get a proper look at her.

"It is how you relate to your family and how you go about building a unit. I look back over my life and I can honestly say that the happiest times of my life have been shared with them."

Terry is running along with bag, microphone and papers. He's panting, struggling to keep up. Stick to the bath-time interviews, old man.

"William Lyon Phelps said it: 'The highest happiness on earth is in marriage. Every man who is happily married is a successful man, even if he has failed in everything else'."

Kay looks over at me happily running alone, wrapped in my thoughts. She catches my eye. "I love you," she mouths. What a special birthday I am having!

We have just run over a bridge in a valley and have to dig into the steep pull on the other side. The thirty-two-kilometre mark is in sight, and I see Inyathi, not as a great Zulu *isangoma* or *impi*, but as a sore, tired runner like the rest of us. I know why he is here today. He came to learn from me.

Inyathi, real courage comes now. It is not a fierce duel between mind and body. Many think courage to see the race to the end is developing a steel-like mind that overcomes the pain we feel; but it is not. Yield now, and travel within yourself. You were sent to me to re-find the courage you have lost, and this is the only place you will find it.

Do not think that courage is the absence of fear, my friend. It is not. Courage to run this race to the end is not a strong, masculine quality. Rather it is a feminine quality that knows how to yield to the pain and fatigue.

Take my hand now, Great Buffalo, and run this hill with

me. It is here that you will defeat your greatest enemy. The man who can defeat his enemies in battle is strong indeed, but Inyathi, the man who can defeat himself is invincible. Run, Inyathi. The time for great courage is now and I will hold your hand.

Oh, Great Buffalo, this is our journey and we will not give up. This is the start of a very long marathon, not its end.

The final stages of the Buffalo Marathon are brutal. Tired legs negotiate their way through impatient Saturday morning shoppers. As I dig deep into my own resources, my ankle is really beginning to hurt. Kay, faithfully from behind, shows concern. "Hey, Tom, you are limping, don't you want to walk a little?"

"I am not done yet, today I shall finish." This is a battle, I think of the last man home, the fallen. How dramatic it is to cheer that brave soldier on, as he struggles to the finish line.

A group of young soldiers, survivors of the Great War, started the Comrades Marathon. One man in particular, Vic Clapham, himself a survivor of the savage horror of the "War to end all wars", put together a race to honour his friends, fallen in battle. And so the Comrades Marathon provides us the opportunity to give dignified expression to our pain and suffering, for both runners and those who watch the race.

Notice how we all honour that last man home before cut-off time, the one who has suffered the most, the one who has endured the longest. We all find meaning in that last hero, but there is more. The camera keeps rolling and we watch the first athlete come in to the stadium after the cut-off gun has been fired. That runner will go home tonight having endured even more than the very last runner home in time, but leaves the race empty-handed. No medal for this soldier. He is the fallen one.

Yet this soldier will rise up on another day. This is the soldier who lives in the very pit of my stomach. In my suffering and defeat lies the seed of this one's brave call. The fallen soldier lives in the essence of my fear, haunts my sleepless nights, stabs where it hurts most. I know I am more complete with this fallen soldier at my side. And so I bite down hard and move on to the end.

The hills around the stadium are steep, and they require a special effort to get to the finish. I am sore, I am done. I yield for the first time in the race and I walk. But thankfully, mercifully, the end comes into view, the music blares, the sun shines and the finish banner flops cheerfully in a stiff coastal breeze.

"Well done, love. One down, five to go. You were so quiet the whole way, are you okay?"

"Yes, thanks Kay. Thanks for running with me."

I stop my watch at five hours and some change minutes.

There is a relaxed, suburban feel at the finish venue. High on an embankment, it overlooks the famous Buffalo Park Cricket Ground. Runners mingle, families relax, and children run around kicking balls. The clouds have lifted and it looks as though the afternoon will be a splendid affair. I sit on the grass and enjoy a well-earned beer. That is when I spot Inyathi leaving the grounds. "Makos, my lord, thank you." He touches his forehead in salute and disappears.

"Kay, did you see that Zulu guy that ran with us?"

"What Zulu guy?"

Inyathi, Great Buffalo, your spirit will be with me on my pilgrimage.

CHAPTER 6

Europe

Stories and the development of our minds

———o0o———

Five years have passed since I said goodbye to Sally, and there is a sad sense of *déjà vu* as the Jumbo lifts into the night sky bound for London. This time I am alone on my own private pilgrimage. I am still haunted by the rolling tragedy of both Risto's and Sally's death. Absently I flip through the in-flight magazine, but the fragrance that was hers, her essence is still with me. I pray that that I will find redemption.

Then I look across the plane and I see her sitting nearby. Sally smiles at me and waves, "Don't be sad, Tom. Life is life, enjoy it to the full. Love everyone that comes to your door and never part in anger from your loved ones, for you never know — this may be your last act."

*   *   *

I had seen this stranger a number of times before. He was following me around, and he wasn't even making it a secret. We made eye contact once or twice, and I knew he had been looking for me.

I had run a testing half marathon in late March, just to make sure that I was still fit. My legs responded well, and I was feeling confident about the upcoming race in London. Sunday morning, and I was in good spirits. I walked around the finish venue sipping a Coke, and — there he was again! This was a good time to make an introduction. I walked up and stood in front of the stranger.

He would have stood out in any crowd. He looked like I would imagine Plato to have looked, with snow-white hair, a white beard, and robed in a white sheet — an ancient toga. His eyes were clear, not brown but not green either. Eyes of intelligence.

"Hi, my name is Tom, you've been following me."

My statement hung between us. The man looked up and held my gaze. He didn't blink and it felt like time stood still. I am not sure how long I stood there in front of him — but it seemed like a long, long time.

"My name is Zeno, and I have been sent here to teach you."

His voice had a deep timbre to it that carried rich warmth. There was a slight hint of an accent. Greek, Italian, perhaps even Spanish, I could not tell. Certainly Mediterranean.

"What have you come to teach me?"

"Whatever you want to learn. I am not sure why, but you are a 'special assignment'."

"Whoa. You had better back up a bit here, Cousin Zeno. Help me out, you have been following me around, and now you tell me you are here to teach me something, you're not sure what. Let me ask a few questions, like who sent you?"

"The Universe sent me. Because you called out to the Greatness — and you expected an answer."

"I did?"

"... and I am Zeno — long before your time. You may have read of me? I started the school of philosophy called the Stoics."

I had read something about the Stoics, but I was more interested in Zeno himself.

"You heard my call? What did I say to the Universe?" I have known weirdness before, but this ...

"You are searching in the depth and in the height, but you are clear and honest in your calling, so it is I who am here. Thinkers like Seneca and Marcus Acreullius followed me. They too called out. No life should go unexamined. So here I am, and the discussion we have is about no small matter, but rather on the right way to live our lives. So now the Universe says 'sit at my Porch'."

"Tom, hey Tom, what is wrong? Why are you staring at the ground, is there something wrong?" Kay put an arm around me, concern in her eyes.

"No, I'm fine, everything is fine."

Zeno was gone. In the car park I saw an old man with white hair disappear into the crowd.

"I'm losing it — but I'm fine."

I dug around in books long since forgotten. The Stoics. I needed to know more. I found they were not part of the mainstream philosophy. Stoa is the Ancient Greek word for "porch". Zeno was their founder but he did not have enough money to place his school inside the Atrium, so he was forced to teach outside, on the porch.

It would be a mistake to believe that the basic teaching of the Stoics was akin to a stiff upper lip and a hard sucked-in stomach. Stoics were closer to Zen Buddhists. They have a certain quiet detachment from the circumstances of the world. The Stoic focuses on inner calm and peace, regardless of outer turmoil. The philosopher's mind turns inward to a world of quiet and tranquillity. This is the point. That is perhaps what Zeno had come to teach! It is the same with running a marathon. In the place of "magical miles" towards the end of the race, the runner enters the mind of the Stoic.

Zeno was a patient teacher with a quick laugh and an even quicker wit. I felt so stupid next to him. Early one evening I went for a training run on a testing hill near my house. I sprinted to the top, and looked down over the evening enveloping the northern suburbs of Johannesburg. Zeno was there.

"I want to tell you a story that will become important on your pilgrimage," he said.

Old Jed was not a wealthy man, nor was he poor. Jed recognised his wealth in the things around him, and more importantly, the people around him — his family and his friends. Jed lived outside a small village on top of a small hill. While he did not get too involved with the people of the village, he was nevertheless loved, and the people loved his company when he came to town to trade and buy his monthly provisions.

Jed was a keen horseman and also a breeder. Every spring he would bring a new foal to town and sell it to one of the townsfolk. Life was peaceful for this mild-mannered man.

One day, to Jed's complete and utter amazement, a young horse walked up the hill to the homestead and just stood there. The villagers were amazed. They assembled and walked to Jed's home to share in his good fortune. "Oh Jed," they cried. "Is this not the best of fortunes? A new steed has come to stay with you, you didn't even have to buy him."

"Who knows," said Jed, "if this is good luck or if it is bad luck?"

The villagers looked perplexed, and laughed as they walked down the hill. "Old Jed, he is a strange one."

A few days after the new horse arrived, it walked out of Jed's homestead. All the mares followed the horse and disappeared. Jed was now just as perplexed as the villagers.

They came up the hill to commiserate with Old Jed. "Oh Jed," they said, "What are you going to do? All of your mares have gone with that strange horse."

"Well," said Jed, "I am not sure what to do, but who knows if this is good luck, or if it is bad luck?"

The villagers looked at each other and looked at Jed, and they were perplexed. They left Jed's home, and laughed as they walked down the hill.

One night as Jed was getting ready for bed, he heard a noise outside. In the yard were a great number of horses. All his mares had returned, as well as the new stranger. With them there were at least a dozen other steeds.

Presently the villagers heard about Jed's latest good fortune. They were happy for the kindly man, and they gathered in his yard.

"Oh Jed," they cried, "is this not the most amazing good fortune?"

Jed looked over the crowd, and they fell silent.

"This may look like good fortune, but who knows if this is good luck or if it is bad luck?"

Again the villagers walked down the hill laughing to one another. "Surely we know that Jed is an odd fruit."

Jed was secretly pleased with his good fortune, and he decided to break the new horses in, for they were still wild. For this task he used his eldest son who was strong and fearless, but had a quiet and loving nature that the horses seemed to trust.

One day as they were working, Jed's son fell from a horse and broke his leg. The villagers made their way up the well-worn path. "Old Jed," they cried, "we are so sorry for your poor son." The kindly man replied, "His leg is broken, it is true — but who knows if this is good luck or if it is bad luck?"

The villagers were amazed and looked at each other. When they had all shaken Jed's hand and patted him on the shoulder, they left. As they walked down the hill, they laughed. "Old Jed, he is a strange one."

Then the land where Jed lived was plunged into war with its neighbours. Each and every able-bodied citizen of a certain age was forced by the king to join the army and go out and fight.

Jed's son was still recovering from his fall and could not go to war. When the villagers heard this, they were overjoyed for Jed. They made the journey up the hill to the house. "Oh Jed, your son has been spared from certain death. Are you not happy?"

Jed looked over the crowded courtyard, and a stillness fell over them.

"It is true, my dear friends, my son has been spared, and for that I am grateful," said Jed, "but who knows if this is good luck or if it is bad luck?"

Once again the villagers were perplexed — and they laughed as they walked down the hill, for Jed, they concluded, was a very strange man.

That day I did not go down the hill with the villagers, but decided to stay on the mountaintop and learn something of Jed. As I sat watching the sun set over the courtyard, there was a stillness and peace about the place.

Presently Jed came and sat next to me, and there was a long silence. We looked over the valley, over the village, to the fields beyond the houses.

"Those people will never understand," said Jed staring at the ground in front of him. "If we must depend on the things around us and the events that take place to give us our happiness, we will never know joy."

"Happiness and joy, and even peace, is a state of mind. More than that, it is a state of being. I do not know what will happen next, but whatever it is — it is neither good luck nor bad luck."

Zeno had made his point.

In the clear, sweet evening I ran down the hillside. I felt a peace I had never felt before. Old Jed watched, and somehow I understood that the spirits of Old Jed and his horses will follow me wherever I go. There is more meaning on the hillside of Old Jed's homestead, with its horses, than there is on any cluttered mantelpiece full of medals and trinkets.

* * *

So with the company and guidance of Zeno, my Teacher, I arrive at these words:

The word I would place on a page
The word I would write in the sand
The word I would have on my headstone
The one word — that is the purest expression of my life —
Is there one word that could sum up all?
No! I wish it were that simple.
My life is made of symphonies and guitar riffs.
My life is made of wild explosive orgasms and anguish and despair.
My life is made up of tastes of chilli and potato skins.
I strut on a stage like a rock star — and
I sit on the toilet holding my head.
My life has felt the victory of childbirth and the failure of an exam.
I have painted a picture and I have painted a kitchen wall.
I have walked — a white boy in a black crowd — I have held a black friend at a white funeral.
Is there a word for this? Is there a sound or a note for it?
Can one put a sketch to this? Or sculpt a shape of this — I think not. For this is A LIFE!

Once I thought that the word written in the sand, the one on the empty page would be "be" or even "love".

Does a word help me deal with beggars at a traffic light?

There is no word that describes the fear of a loving father riding on the Awesome Cobra, just to please his daughter.

* * *

"And so Tom, how has your training been going for London?"

"Terry, it has gone well. Since Buffalo I have been applying the principle of good rest, with hard training. I am fitter now than I was for Buffalo."

"I had a life-changing training run last Sunday — you want to hear about it?"

"I'm sure the listeners do, Tom."

I have been having problems with the national athletics body, and it looks ugly. I have been worried as it could mean a bitter and costly court battle."

"Gee, Tom, how did you get into such a position?"

"It is long and complicated. I'm a victim of circumstance. I am reaping a whirlwind not of my own making. Anyway, about this Sunday's run, I set out to do a long one, and was well prepared mentally for a good five hours alone. But I have been having sleepless nights. I have been waking in the cold, small hours of the morning, and I see a pack of wolves baying for my blood.

"I went out on this Sunday morning run in a poor state, I must tell you Terry, in a poor state indeed. My stomach was in a knot, I hadn't slept and I was exhausted.

"Early in the run I could think of every excuse to cut short. I had a sleepless night, so I was tired — right? I could go home and phone an advocate friend. I should be at home worrying, not out there on the road training.

"Then a small, still voice inside said, 'You owe it to yourself to train, you are far greater than the sum of all of your problems, Tom. You owe this to yourself.' I began to run with a spring in my step, I ran with strength. The longer I ran, the stronger I got. The legal problems, the shortage of money, the weight of my load lightened, step by step and stride by stride.

"The training run was punishing, but I returned with a sense of purpose and peace. I connected with the deep will and hope that resides in my spirit. I was not afraid. I think, for the first time in my life, I am beginning to really understand what it's all about.

Terry nodded.

"I learned that no matter the circumstance, no matter what people say, or think or even do, nothing can destroy the essential runner that I am. Running is an extension of my being. That essence exists independent of my current circumstances. Our daily activity is close to the great parable of the run. How we perform at top level in the boardroom or in a high-powered sales presentation, is the same as we perform in the big race. The principles of Big Match Temperament are the same. It is all about BMT.

"Independent of whatever else is happening, the great athlete focuses everything on the desired outcome. The one who succeeds is the one who desires it the most. The essence of a great and successful life is to harness this belief and extend it into each hour, each minute of our activity. This is what I learned on my run on Sunday, pretty good huh?"

Terry was gone, the radio was playing and Kay was hooting in the driveway — oh well — upwards and onwards into the day.

* * *

Zeno stood alone and sometimes aloof. He was at the end of many training runs and local races. His was always a voice of reason, but it was more than that. It was soft, calm, and came from a place that was uncluttered. His was the voice of simplicity.

Whenever I needed to hear the settled working of my own mind, it was Zeno, the father-like figure who was listening and who softly spoke. "Make the journey, my young apprentice, make the journey from your head to your heart." His eyes reflected a depth of knowledge and understanding that few had plumbed. In his smile lay more than a thousand years of wisdom.

"And knowledge, what is that? Knowledge is power. With knowledge a man can reach the stars, search the universe. With knowledge we can save a child, we can save a planet. But knowledge is not enough; it is only with experience and love that we form the strength of knowledge into the power of wisdom."

* * *

Zeno told of Reason and Passion.

Two sons were given a vineyard to run. The one, Passion, was impetuous and rowdy but he had many ideas and got on well with the farm workers.

The other, Reason, was good at business, but was quiet and reserved. While the two brothers loved each other, their ways were very different.

When the time came for the first harvest, Reason was overjoyed, for the yield would be bountiful. The grapes were rich and round, and the crop would yield a good return.

At this important time Passion, whose job it was to organise the picking teams, was nowhere to be found. Reason tried to find and harness the teams himself, but he could not do it. He was too far removed from the people. He did not even know where to begin.

During the harvest week it began to rain and soon all opportunity for harvesting was lost. About a week later, Passion came to the door of Reason. Reason looked him up and down with an icy stare, "Where have you been?"

"I was at the market place," declared Passion with pride. "I have found many new buyers for our grapes as well as our wine."

They looked at each other, both with disappointment in their hearts. Reason blamed Passion for the loss of their harvest. Passion was at a loss, for surely Reason could have organised a simple thing while he was away on important farm business?

It was at this impasse that Zeno intervened.

"Come," he implored the two brothers. "Let us go to the harbour."

The three sat in silence on the harbour wall. In the bay was a brigantine hove-to, and Zeno pointed to the ship now tacking its way to the mouth.

"See how sail and rudder work so magnificently to bring the ship safely to harbour? See how the sails, now set to the full, propel the ship through the water? See too, how the skilful pilot steers the ship on a safe course?

"The sails of a ship represent the passion and driving force. But beware — passion alone will drive any good ship onto the rocks. It is also true that the rudder and steerage represent reason. But what use is reason alone? No matter how much steering is done, without passion the ship will never even leave the harbour."

The two brothers understood. Reason embraced Passion, and from that day on the wine farm truly prospered.

* * *

Zeno has always been the quiet voice of reason, balancing my passion. Zeno is the Great Philosopher and Great Teacher in my life. He was with me on my first day of school; he was with me when I graduated from university.

As you think, so you create your reality, he teaches. And I have come to hold this truth. Be aware of your thoughts, for they shall become your reality. Your thoughts are the most powerful driving force in your life. Whatever your mind decides, and thinks — it is right.

I love the instruction Zeno gives me: clear, simple, logical. Zeno is serious, he is kind and gentle — but there is a fierce and independent strength within. He reminds me of Obi-Wan Kenobi, the Jedi knight from *Star Wars*.

When Zeno gives a discourse, it is best to pay close attention.

You like to meditate? He asks. Well then follow this instruction. Get comfortable. Clear your mind of all the clutter. Breathe and relax. Now, in your mind, float above your physical being. Observe yourself in this meditative state. Observe the room and yourself in it. See how comfortably you fill this room with your presence. Now ask yourself this: Who is it that is meditating? Answer that, Tom, and you are on the way to understanding the essence of your being.

And so it is with Zeno, I have many discourses on the working of the mind. Want to know what your horoscope is for tomorrow? Think carefully about the thoughts you had yesterday, and that is your future.

Guard carefully thought, word and deed. Discipline your mind thus, and you can have any future you want.

Zeno stabs the air. His eyes twinkle with the intelligent sparkle of a crystal clear pond on a cold winter's morning. He places his hand on my shoulder. Your actions will create your habits, and your habits will become the blocks that build your future. Your future will become your destiny. So give serious thought to your thoughts.

* * *

How sublime it is to be in England. I sit on a bench in Hyde Park, the sky shell-pink. A sign asks me not to disturb the wildlife. Wildlife? A duck on the pond, and nearby a motley squirrel peers nervously at me from behind a bed of red and yellow tulips. Two of England's Big Five?

England is a gentle place. The green is really green and the sky is pastel. There is a chill in the air — it is spring but there is a wintry bite. People are gentle and reserved, polite in queues. They are a people I feel close to and at home with. Does one say they are quirky? They are my kin.

The contrast between the London Marathon and the Buffalo Marathon cannot be any starker. This race is the biggest in Europe and perhaps even in the world. There are over 30 000 starters, split between three different venues. There are over five million spectators lining the route, and the race is televised worldwide.

The din at the start is enormous. It is freezing cold, the rain is being driven in by a howling gale, and I am apprehensive about the grey clouds above. A tall, thin athlete shakes my hand: "Welcome, South Africa, have a good run. Beautiful day for a marathon, what do you say?"

I look at this man and wonder if he is moral. Moral? Yes, moral — for an Englishman thinks he is moral only when he is uncomfortable. That's George Bernard Shaw for you. I try to huddle in my makeshift raincoat, my black rubbish bag made in South Africa, trying not to get wet. This guy is dressed for a hot African summer's day, raindrops dripping from his blue nose, and smiling. Maybe we do come from different worlds.

The mass moves forward. Great excitement. Difficult to find a good stride because the road is jam-packed and barriers line the entire route. The spectators stand five deep, under brollies and great overcoats.

"Go South Africa — Go Holland — Morning New Zealand."

Near me runs a petite blonde girl with a Russian flag on her vest.

Zeno draws near — "Hey Howzit — you running for Greece?" Zeno smiles and quotes Socrates: "I am a citizen, not of Athens or Greece, but of the world." Too true, my mentor — my sentiment exactly.

Parts of the race are larger than life. The Cutty Sark is moored in the middle of the tide of boiling humanity. There are mad dogs and Englishmen everywhere. No midday sun, but the atmosphere is festive.

There is an exuberance and a feeling of great joy as I run; a feeling that mind, body and spirit are indeed working as a unified whole. My heart wants to sing, my body feels strong, and all my senses are alive. I stand in this moment and I scream with unrestrained joy — the crowd roars back — Zeno stands there and claps his hands and laughs.

There are no hills on this race. The Tower Bridge is the only challenge. Running this marathon is like taking a guided tour of the city. The one tricky part is on the Embankment outside the Tower of London. Here, the ancient cobbles, laid centuries ago, form part of the route. It is a difficult part of the course that needs to be warily negotiated. Still, the organisers have placed a fine red carpet over the cobbles, and this helps a little.

As Big Ben comes into sight, I know the end is near. Ahead is a disciplined company of British paratroopers in full battle dress complete with backpack. Nice one, guys. Insane way to run a marathon.

A sergeant tells me they are going to Iraq in a month's time and this is their final fitness test.

The finish of this great race is in front of Buckingham Palace. I am cold, I am tired, and I am sore. But my mentor for this part of the journey is there. Zeno smiles. "The more a man finds his sources of pleasure in himself, the happier he will be." Zeno touches his nose knowingly, nodding acknowledgement as I collect my medal in the pouring rain. "The highest, most varied and lasting pleasures are those of the mind." The words of Arthur Schopenhaur.

I am a grinning old man standing at the Palace Gate. I have my treasure. Even in death it will be mine. I wink at Zeno and he disappears. My stopwatch reads 05:11:27.

CHAPTER 7

Australasia

The value of friendship

——o0o——

The Maori word *hau* commonly means wind. More subtly, it refers to the part of a person that is left behind where they have sat or walked. Consider the faint waft of a breeze as we pass each other in the corridor. The scent you leave behind as you make passage through your busy day. The warmth of the body that remains after a person has left a chair.

One of the most important blessings of my pilgrimage was the renewal of old friendships around the world. When in London for the marathon, I was with a tour group and lucky enough to be staying within easy walking distance of the British Museum. I could have spent my time exploring the museums, galleries or just taking in the vibrant energy that is London. But even better, I could surround myself with the friendship of an old comrade and his family; renew my acquaintance with old friends, Alfie and Judy.

I had hugged them both and watched them depart from my life more than ten years ago. I was not sure if I would still recognise them. I phoned Alfie and arranged to meet him at the hotel.

"Bugger this place, I want to come and stay with you, see your family."

"Hang in there, Tom, it will take me a while, but I am coming."

I was waiting in the lobby when suddenly Alfie was there! A bit greyer but as big and as warm as the day we had said goodbye in South Africa.

Before long, I was in Judy's pub with a frothy ale, looking across a table at old friends smiling back and caring about me. I knew that my visit might leave the cold, yet interesting halls of learning and curiosity empty. Here my spirit sat at that table with kindred ones and together we roamed the day-to-day and the humdrum. Such an occasion is priceless. Wherever in the world I may be, when I am with friends, I am home.

I knew that my trip to New Zealand would also be special. I was going to stay with Al and Eva. Add to that the prospect of renewing contact with many other South African friends who had settled there, and in truth I was excited.

But I was also anxious. So far I had run a marathon in early March, and another in mid-April. Now it was the end of April, and the New Zealand Rotorua Marathon was on May 1. My training had been sporadic at best. I had hardly run since London, but that had been deliberate. I had been scared that I might catch a cold after such bitter, wet weather, so I pampered myself.

As a pilgrim on a mission I could afford only the cheapest travelling option: fly to Auckland via Dubai. Talk about being saddle-sore. Over thirty hours in transit and God knows how many time zones. Still, I made the flight, Eva met me at the airport, and I was among friends.

Later that night, the dinner party could have been taking place anywhere in the world at any time. The last time I had a meal with these folk had been ten years ago, back in South Africa. But as we ate and drank there was a glow of love around that table. There was a timeless quality that bonded us. It was spaceless, seamless. We had all aged a little, but we picked up the conversation in mid-sentence.

These friends came to New Zealand to find a different way of life. Some were afraid of the turning tide in a South Africa teetering on revolution. Some came to the island for a new adventure. All had left a hole in my life back home. But here we were, the bonds between us never broken. Such is the nature and the strength of friendship.

The spirit we bear does not wait for our death to become spirit, for it is with us right from birth. Wherever we have gone before, we have left the scent of our being, the faint whisper of our breeze. This is a subtle and yet profound understanding typical of the people of this land. And so it was with these friends who had left their vital wind essence of spirit — their *hau* — at my dinner table all those years ago.

The purpose of friendship is "the deepening of the spirit", says Kahlil Gibran. "In the sweetness of friendship let there be laughter, and sharing of pleasures. For in the dew of the little things, the heart finds its morning and is refreshed."

* * *

Taina ("Junior" in Maori) was chosen to formally give me greeting and to teach me on this part of my pilgrimage. I first met this young, scrawny and featureless lad for less than three seconds. It happened while I was running the marathon. All the runners around me were warning of the monster hill up ahead. "It's a real bugger, mate, just take it slow." Sagely local advice. There stood next to the twenty-six-kilometre marker board, at the base of the hill.

"*Kia-ora,*" he yelled as I ran past.

A fellow runner roughly translated: "Strength to you."

The Maori youth pressed a letter into my hand. I leaned into the hill and looked down. I have done this so many times before, what hill in Rotorua could break my spirit? The challenge was there.

Much later, in the cocooned anonymity of the flight home, I read the letter. It confirmed the truth I held on friendship. But Taina's letter went further: "We welcome you here *Pakeha*, strange white man, to the Land of the Long White Cloud. Welcome from afar *manuhiri tuarangi*, our distinguished guest.

"In our welcome to our sacred place we put before you our challenge, here in Rotorua. We open this *pohiri*, this welcoming ceremony, knowing the rituals and observances are *tapu*, spiritual in nature. We are mindful of the great distances you have travelled. We are also mindful of your spiritual journey, your ancestors will bless your quest.

"Our challenge to you is the road you see before you. It is twenty miles of hope, followed by six miles of truth. Do you pick up this challenge? To help you on your trail we will send to you a friend to be at your side — a companion, a guide, your strength, help and inspiration.

"We thank you for your presence at our *marae*, our ceremonial courtyard, and we will be happy to teach you our customs and traditions. No man stands alone on the soft earth and in the cool air, so we want to teach you of the place of our home.

"Here we assemble before you, as many of our warriors have assembled on our rugby fields in the past. It is our great tradition to open any auspicious contest with our war dance, the *haka*. We regard your presence for this race as important."

The *haka* is a frightening challenge. The performers' faces are fierce and there is electricity in the air. The group pulls down hard with their arms, bringing to them the potency of their rich ancestral life. There is nothing subtle about the challenge of the *haka*. I stood with arms folded, not flinching. Twenty miles of hope, six miles of truth — the challenge was mine.

The cabin is in darkness, most of the other passengers are asleep. I switch on the overhead light and continue to read Taina's letter. "It seems fitting then that both of us, host and guest, have prepared well for this *pohiri*, this welcoming meeting. You will run around our lake called Rotorua. We are mindful that you have prepared yourself in mind and body for this ordeal. It brings us to a state of *noa*, where we are relaxed and we know that host and guest are well pleased with each other's presence. Our prayer and our hope this day is that we can close this challenge with the words '*i puta te ihi*'. We hope that the performances this day are brilliant and exhilarating."

The small TV screen at the back of the seat in front flickers as the passenger next to me soundlessly watches a movie, headphones on, blanket pulled up to her chin. I return to Taina's letter.

"Visitor to this place, *Pakeha*, we wish you take home learning and understanding, not of us and our ways, but a better understanding of yourself.

"Know this, that our challenge is firstly twenty miles of hope. We ask you a simple but direct question — what is your hope?"

I put down the letter and stare out of the window as the plane speeds home above the clouds. My hope?

I have great hopes for myself on this voyage. I hope I can record all of this in a clear and loving way. I fully expect to grow in this year, spiritually and mentally. To arrive at the end of my journey fit and strong in body. To renew friendships lost in time and space. To make a difference in my community.

My life has always been about myself and my family. My hope is now different; it is about Myself, my greater Self. To be a bigger, more loving and rounded person. To express well my love and my gratitude. To walk among my peers, a giant. I wish to stride this world with the self-confidence of a hero. My hope is to call myself "athlete", "academic", "lover" and "friend", and to know that I am so. To become a more complete human being. In Maori terms, I seek to find my *mana* — my bearing as a human being.

"*Pakeha* — you have hopes for your *mana*. We do too. May your bearing and your presence increase as you journey around the world. Your *mana* is the personal prestige you display; may yours be great. As you pass from the room, may we feel your wind as you leave. May the print you leave behind on your seat remain, and may it be warm. May your shadow still be cast, even in an empty room.

"Make no mistake, the hopes you carry in your heart are the hopes of all men. In this marathon challenge, we will also present you with six miles of truth. So we ask you, *Pakeha*, what is your simple truth?"

I put aside the letter while a meal is served. The airhostess jostles with an unwieldy cabinet bearing our pre-packed meals — "Beef or Chicken?" Oh please — give me a break.

My truth? My truth is that I am scared. I feel less than a match for my hopes. My truth is that I'm not sure of anything, and that I am weak. If I were to stand before the Eternal Court, could I give a worthy account of my life? Sometimes it is easier to hide from truth in an anaesthetised, alcoholic state. While the outer package of hope is big, brazen and apparently confident, the inner package is but a shadow of its noisy cousin.

Know then the truth, and the truth shall set you free. I gulp down the last mouthful of wine and return to my letter.

"Truth is always a harder path to follow than hope. That is why in our marathon challenge we give you the last six miles only after some testing. It is here that we will show you to yourself. Truth is our way of teaching you *tapu*. *Tapu* is everywhere, it is present in people, places, buildings, things and even in words.

"As your *mana* grows in strength, so does your *tapu*. Go through this life and breathe strength into your truth. Walk with great respect through the world, run with reverence for all things, for here is the essence of truth. You are more than what your body is, you are greater than your own mind.

"Your *tapu* is not made up only of simple physical elements. The shadow of your truth is greater than this, and in it, your spirit moves. You are afraid of your truth, *Pakeha*. You are without boundary or restraint. Your truth is limitless and without fear.

"It is friendship that binds us one to another and makes us strong. You bring with you your *hau*, your wind. *Pakeha*, this we take to be your spirit of life, you bring this to us and we welcome you as family and as friend. Your *hau* is your vitality, this you breathe into all your relations, it is this wind that you leave with us, and we become brothers and sisters."

The whisper, the slight breeze I feel as the hostess passes me on the way to the back of the craft startles me. I am suddenly aware of both her presence and Taina's.

I put down the letter and stare long and hard into the night.

* * *

Of course the race in Rotorua was washed out. Why shouldn't it be? After all it had rained in Africa, it had pissed in Europe, and now this, driving rain in New Zealand. Break the drought. Get me to go on a pilgrimage anywhere. Rent the Rainman.

My host and close friend, Al, kept me company during the race. He really didn't have to; he is a well-trained athlete, not a plodding pilgrim with a bad limp. He is a man of high spirits, with not a grumpy bone in his body. He has the running style of boisterous puppy-dog, full of boundless energy. Al is a great inspiration and lots of fun on the run.

We trotted along happily, Al making all the insane comments a runner can make. We joined a big group of runners from the local YMCA club, all decked out in yellow vests. We sloshed through a watering table.

"Mind if we join the Yellow Submarine?"

"Hi mate, you from South Africa?"

"Yea, and don't mention the rugby, don't mention the cricket, in fact no, I'm from Mozambique."

It was pouring with rain. Al had humoured me, chatted with me, and harangued me for almost thirty kilometres. I could see that he was getting impatient. He was a much stronger runner than I and he wanted to finish his race and get out of the rain and the wind. Friendship stretches far — but there is a breaking point. He grabbed my hand, gave it a squeeze and ran on, bounding along in puppy-dog fashion. I watched him disappear into the bobbing crowd of runners ahead.

He and Eva waited patiently for me as I crossed the soggy finish line. The clock at the side glowed in the gloom. 05:12:07. I felt pleased with myself. In terms of the number of races to be completed on my pilgrimage, I was at the halfway mark. I was tired, really tired. Still, consistent times were good. Slow but consistent. I had earned the right to be the five hour pilgrim.

* * *

The hardest thing about the matric Latin class was the humiliation and sheer terror of being picked on by Klev, the Latin master.

Most of those in Sydney Kelevensky's classes were pupils, I was a customer. It was because of him that I saw more of the inside of a detention classroom than I did the inside of the rugby change-room.

As he spat out declensions and conjugations, my eyes roamed the walls of this small man's classroom. He would rant and rave like a Roman general before a battle with Carthage. He would stamp and shout, and then point at me: "You, Cottrell, are a sad disappointment. If you cannot spend some time learning the simple rules of Latin, you will never amount to anything."

I often wondered why I had ever taken Latin in the first place. Klev's classes were torturous; he was worse than the playground bully. But it was because of Ovid and Pliny and Cicero that I wanted to study Latin, not Klev.

Recently I picked up a book, well translated, of the writings of Cicero. I felt as if Cicero was talking directly to me. He was my teacher then, he is my teacher now. He writes to his friend Scipio in the senectute, a great philosophical treatise on his ideas of growing old.

"I suppose that you hear, Scipio, what your grandfather's host, Masinnissa, is doing at this day, at the age of ninety ... There is in him the greatest hardiness of frame; and therefore he performs all his duties and functions like that of a king. Exercise, therefore, and temperance, even in old age, can preserve some remnant of our pristine vigour.

"We must make a stand against old age, and its faults must be atoned for by activity. We must fight, as it were, against disease, and in like manner against old age. Regard must be paid to health; moderate exercises must be adopted; so much of meat and drink must be taken that the strength may be recruited, not oppressed. Or, in deed, not only must the body alone be supported, but also the mind and the soul much more; for these also, unless you drop oil on them as on a lamp, they are extinguished by old age ... Our minds are rendered buoyant by exercise.

"As I like a young man in whom there is something of the old, so I like an old man in whom there is something of the young, and he who follows this maxim will possibly be an old man in body, but he will never be an old man in mind.

"Intelligence, reflection and judgment reside in old men. Age, especially an honoured old age, has so great authority that this is of more value than all the pleasures of youth. Old age is the consummation of life, just as of a play. The harvest of old age is the recollection and abundance of blessings previously secured. To those who have not the means within themselves of a virtuous and happy life, every age is burdensome."

I took the punishment of Latin so that I could sit at the feet of great thinkers and philosophers. It was never the language itself that held any great attraction for me; it was the great ideas. If I have anything to thank my cruel and belligerent Latin master for, it is for taking me to the very doors of wisdom and bidding me enter.

* * *

Friendship was there at the start of our marriage, and it was with us now as we celebrated our twenty-fifth anniversary. This was a memorable family celebration. The winter chill was outside, but inside was the warmth of a crowded room. Kay and I had hired out the entire restaurant. The room sat quietly, expectantly, waiting for Kay to speak. In the corner a fire crackled with the comfort of good company.

In that pause, time stood still. There is great power in friendship. In that split second lay a lifetime of good company and love. Smells wafted tantalisingly from the kitchen. Waiters stood to attention, serviettes folded across forearms. This moment warmly embraced more than one lifetime of love. In a second, friends became lovers, fences were mended, and eternity was a tiny space where spirits soared. Kay spoke so well about the depth of friendship, and I knew, even more than a wife, I had a friend. Then it was Bronwyn's turn.

Bronwyn, our youngest daughter held the floor. Where had this beautiful young woman been hiding? Before us stood a confident, self-assured person who just yesterday was the nursery school terror. The "forest-friend".

Bronwyn has a no-nonsense approach to life. She knows what she wants and she gets it. Kay and I stood holding hands, transformed, as this graceful dancer pouted, strutted, and held an enchanted audience in the palm of her hand. "I have known these two all my life ..." Laughter. She knows how to control a crowd.

In many ways I have difficulty in colourfully weaving Bronwyn into the dramatic fabric of everyday family life. It is not because I love her any less, it is because she is always "there". I now understand those who were left behind when the prodigal son marched off to find fortune. Bronwyn is like that to me; just like that. "So now I would like to propose a toast to my parents ..."

She smiles, holding a glass up to the ceiling. "To Mom and Dad, our best friends." Neither time nor space nor generations can separate friends from one another.

* * *

The closing weeks of Comrades training are particularly challenging and rewarding. Challenging because of the onset of winter. The dark and frosty mornings in late May and early June are always a test, even for the hardiest. Rewarding, because the end is near, and the bonding with fellow athletes takes on almost spiritual dimensions.

One morning, two weeks before the Comrades Marathon, it

seemed a lot colder, and the effort required to arrive at the training session even more intense. Still, my running partner, Christopher, was there. Our pact still intact.

Our conversation over the past few months had centred on Christopher's divorce and his children. The family home had been sold, his ex-wife was living in Durban, and he was having trouble getting access to his children. All I could do was listen patiently to his plight. This was heavy going, and I wished to find some silver lining in these dark and cheerless mornings.

It happened by surprise. Christopher's proverbial silver lining came along one day in the form of a young, lively and beautiful flautist from the national orchestra. Carolyn was no athlete, but Christopher adored her, and for our group of hardy runners, that was enough to place her centre-stage.

At the start of each Comrades, the massive sea of bobbing heads passes by the TV cameras. A fine opportunity for grabbing fifteen seconds of fame, and to make a statement — if you wish. And so with TV was born a Comrades tradition: banners, posters and balloons with messages to loved ones at home.

"Ma — it's me", "Howzit Bethal", and "Jesus Saves".

Christopher was not above such cheap advertising, and the previous year he had carefully prepared a gigantic poster in which he publicly confessed his love for Carolyn. Would he repeat the performance this year? My man Christopher had a plan.

With all the starting rituals dispensed with, and the gun duly fired by an important official with a chain around his neck, we bobbed our way into the sunrise. Christopher then held up his carefully written poster. "Carolyn — will you marry me?" I looked at the poster and then at the insane look on his face. I knew this demented man was serious.

"Hey man, have you gone completely mad?"

Christopher's eyes were like diamonds and his fixed grin looked scary. "Pretty cool, hey?"

A disc jockey at a radio station in Johannesburg caught his sign on TV and became intrigued. The camera picked up Christopher's race number and from there it was easy to find out who this romantic idiot was. The enterprising and relentless radio staff tracked down Carolyn, who was studying at the London School of Music.

Soon she was live on radio. She was told of his proposal. She paused, the public gasped, and Carolyn gave her answer. The whole of South Africa knew the answer as my moronic, romantic running mate ran to Durban clutching his poster.

No one was more surprised than Christopher when he ran into the stadium to a standing ovation. Someone pointed to the gigantic cricket screen board.

"Christopher Smith — the answer is Yes! Carolyn."

It took a contingent of three officials to prise the proposal board from his stiff hands so that they could present him with his medal.

There is a happy postscript to this story. I had the honour of being best man for Christopher at their wedding. He and Carolyn are happily married and now live in Oxford. On my wall is a photograph of him running down the Inchanga Bank with an insane grin on his face.

* * *

"In each race I have learned that the desire to quit comes but once. It is a coward that once beaten, does not return."

Not my words, but those of Tim Noakes. I felt the need to quit while in New Zealand. Not just to quit the race, but to throw in the towel and stop this whole project. No more pilgrimage shit.

Al was giving me a lift back to Auckland Airport and we stopped off for a cup of coffee. "Tom, you surprise me. Quit? You? Why?"

I think it happens when you are really tired. It was all beginning to catch up with me. I had run two marathons in as many weeks. I had spent more hours in an airplane than I care to think about. The flights from London, back home to Johannesburg, to Dubai, to Singapore, then Brisbane and to Auckland. I felt vulnerable and was beginning to question the sanity of all of this.

Self doubt runs alongside many who undertake projects and pilgrimages. I wonder if Edmund Hillary ever looked up at the summit of Everest and thought, "This is madness — I can't go through with this".

I sat in a coffee shop with my dear friend Al in New Zealand. He was animated, waving his arms, his message clear. "If you quit now, I will kick your sorry ass all the way back to South Africa. You've been an inspiration to so many people; many have dreams and they don't have the courage to follow through. If you toss in the towel now, you will confirm to hundreds the bland truth — that it is never worthwhile to dream dreams and to act on them. It will become a truth that greatness was never meant for the ordinary man."

The truth is that I felt vulnerable, afraid and even stupid. But for now I would give Al the benefit of the doubt — and believe me, the doubt was big. Huge, in fact.

He dropped me at the airport after his long lecture about giving up. We shook hands and I found my way into the departure lounge. Taina — the young Maori — was at my side as I prepared to leave his land.

"So, did you have a good time here, mate?"

The lilt of his accent was distinctly New Zealand. I looked out over the airplanes parked in the bays; the clouds were rolling in and the city of Auckland was shrouded in mist.

"A good time? I suppose so."

Taina held my hand and looked up at me. "Yes — Taina — thank you, I did have a good time."

Finding the right words is not easy, and giving expression to a life-changing pilgrimage will not be easy. To try to explain why I was thinking of abandoning the quest is even more of a challenge.

When I got home, I took my family out for a pizza. Franco gave me something to think about. Dear Franco was an old friend dating back to our early school days, and now the owner of a popular neighbourhood Italian restaurant. He echoed Al's sentiments. My pilgrimage was beginning to stir hope and dreams in others. I was left with only one choice. I would continue this journey but I must allow myself to acknowledge that it would be difficult at times. There was a warm, friendly hubbub in the restaurant. The smell of garlic, romantic continental music. Franco refilled Kay's wine glass.

"Tom, I have always thought you a little odd, but I never had you down as a quitter."

* * *

Once a prince was sent into the world to find and bring back to the king a great treasure. The treasure was a pearl beyond price. The prince, eager to please, set about his work in earnest, searching for the pearl.

Soon enough the prince was caught up in the day-to-day routine of living. The need to have a home and start a family was a strong call for our hero. To sustain this he felt the need to educate himself in business and to embark on a career. He persevered.

There was an idealistic side to the prince and he gave generously to causes, not only money, but also time. There was an emptiness though. The deeds were done in a mechanical way that gave the prince little meaning. Every now and then he felt a certain fury. The prince didn't really acknowledge it or understand it, but there was an uncomfortable feeling. "Go beyond," a voice called.

The years passed for the prince and agonies visited him.

The loss of his parents, the loss of a friend. One misfortune and then another. Changing jobs, the loss of a job. These seemingly random events came flooding in to the prince's life, undermining his confidence, undermining a well-charted course.

Life had become stale. Children grew up, goals were reached. Only now there was a feeling of incompleteness. Soon enough the prince was forced to ask himself some disturbing questions, and was unable to answer them. He re-examined his attitude to his existence. He believed that it was not so much that he had earned too little, or even that he had loved too much — it was that he had forgotten the reason he was here. He had lost sight of his quest.

And so, one day, the prince remembered the call of the king: "Find and bring to me the pearl." It came as no surprise to the prince that the pearl lay within himself and that he did not have to venture forth to find this great treasure. For, in truth, the pearl was his Soul, now badly in need of repair, but still there. Give up the quest? I am already halfway there.

Before me I see Taina's handwriting. I recall his letter. "Our prayer and our hope this day is that we can close this challenge with the words '*i puta te ihi*'. We hope that the performances this day are brilliant and exhilarating."

Well, Taina, the performances this day truly have been brilliant and exhilarating.

CHAPTER 8

South America

Money and the art of work

———oOo———

An instant of unity and joy. I was out on a training run one freezing June morning when I found myself in the magic of the moment. I was running in a valley close to a river. The air around me was particularly cold, the frost heavy on the ground. Billows of steam rose from the river. The rising sun bathed this icy wonderland in pastel peach light. Training for the marathon in Rio was always going to be difficult, but here, on a wintry Highveld morning, the silent and cold mystery that surrounded this run made it all worthwhile.

I struggled with the onslaught of winter. The hesitancy I had felt in Auckland still lingered, and the creeping self-doubt of my quest ran with me as an unwelcome training partner. It still haunted me, and I remained unsure. The time this was taking and the money I was spending was fertile ground for a fast-growing forest of question marks. Kay kept her council, but I was beginning to suspect that I had overindulged her goodwill, and I was worried that she was growing evermore resentful.

I arrived in South America undertrained and overweight. But bravely, I made the journey and the pilgrimage goes on.

Rio de Janeiro. The hotel I was staying at was a short walk to the Copacabana beach. I sat on a low wall and gazed out to sea, soaking in the humidity and the atmosphere. The beachfront must be at least two kilometres long.

I walked, wrapped in my own thoughts, to the shoreline and felt the water. Nice and warm. I had never seen such a vast expanse of sand on a beach before. With my back to the sea I drank in the expansive sweep of Copacabana. Beyond the volleyball nets lay a six-lane carriageway fringed by a row of hotels, apartments and sidewalk restaurants. The palm trees on the edge of the sand gave the picture an exotic, tropical atmosphere.

It was about nine in the morning and the promenade was already busy, with people walking up and down in droves. There were a number of runners and a few rollerbladers. Everyone looked tanned and healthy; the relaxed atmosphere of Rio is definitely good for one's health. I had arrived the night before, feeling tired and somewhat bewildered. But here I was, standing on a beach on the other side of the world. It was Friday morning.

As the world buzzed by, I felt such a sense of privilege, there on that beach. I know there are many people who would never be able to realise such a dream. Most of the people in South Africa live in such poverty, not only materially, but also spiritually. Many could never have done what I am doing.

The plane had touched down late in the evening. How was I going to get to my hotel? I hardly knew a word of

Portuguese, but this was the least of my worries. Dangerous taxi drivers, wanton theft, and stories of women with loose morals filled my mind. This was thanks largely to armchair traveller friends, who had seldom ventured further than the remote control on the coffee table.

When I stepped out of the customs hall there was no one to meet me, in spite of the travel agent's assurances. As I walked out of the airport I was faced with the noisy choice of over a dozen taxi-drivers vying for my business. I was a little nervous of this rowdy bunch, so I started to scan the crowd for one that looked less than my own fighting weight. Then I saw her. Crowded out by all the rowdy taxi-drivers was a woman.

She was in her mid-thirties with long black hair. She was attractive and much smaller than me. It was the detail that I noticed. Small graceful hands. Dressed in black. Black slacks, a black shirt and a smart pair of black shoes on feet that belonged to a dancer. She had a nametag. Silvia. She stepped forward and took my kit bag.

"*Ola*, I am Silvia, your driver. I am your guide in Rio, come we go now."

This did not surprise me at all. There was a quiet voice in the back of my head. My guide? I know.

We trundled through an empty car park to her taxi, and bundled my bags into the back.

"So, what is your name?"

"Tom."

"And why you here, holiday?"

"Sort of, I've come to run the Rio Marathon on Sunday."

I showed her the paper with the hotel's address and we took off into the night.

"So, okay, you want to see Rio de Janeiro, no?"

"Yes I do, and I must also register for the race. I must get to the Maracana Stadium, do you know where it is?"

"*Si*, I know. I take you there tomorrow."

She dropped me off at my hotel and said goodnight. I watched her drive off. Dangerous taxi-drivers? What the hell was I thinking?

Out at sea there is a large yacht in full sail. On the beach close by, a number of volleyball games are in progress and further up is a soccer game. The pride in Brazil's national game is tangible. Vendors walk up and down the promenade laden with Brazil soccer shirts.

My mind turns to the marathon. I am really worried. If weather forecasts are anything to go by, this race will be the first of my pilgrimage not run in rain. The sky is clear, but it is hot and oppressively humid. This is a race to be tackled with great caution. The plan will be to go out conservatively, drink often and hold back until well into the second half.

I look at my watch. Silvia would pick me up at ten.

* * *

Running is a sport with many public and private rituals. The crowing of the cock that starts the Comrades Marathon is a fine example. This tradition began during the 1930s when an athlete, Max Trimborn, stood on the line and heartily crowed like a cock just before the gun went off. This became a tradition, and he was invited to the start every year to deliver the famous crow. In Max's later years he became frail but the organisers had the presence of mind to record his crow for future generations. To this day, Max blasts forth with gusto, much to the delight and cheers of an appreciative crowd.

Sometimes the ritual is more private and personal. Alan Robb, multiple Comrades winner, always wears a pair of red socks when he runs the race.

Once, a leading runner's mother had a heart attack and died while watching the race. As he ran past it, he wondered why his mother was not at her appointed corner. By that time she was in the ambulance, and had already been pronounced dead. The organisers did not tell him until his race was run. Now, every year he enters the race, they present him with a rose to carry to the spot where his mother died. He drops it there in her memory.

This pilgrimage would be incomplete if I did not craft my own private ritual. It started after my first run, in East London. I went to the beach and picked up three stones off the beach, and so began a small collection.

I have done the same thing at each destination so far. The stones from Europe came from the beach close to Alfie's home; those from Australasia came from Al and Eva's flowerpot in Auckland. Friendship stones. Those from Rio came from a corner of the Copacabana beach.

I pick up three stones because of the symbolic power of the number. Father, Son and Holy Ghost. Past, present and future. Mind, Body and Spirit. In the end I will have three stones each from six continents. I know I will perform a symbolically powerful ritual with such a collection. I am unsure what that act will be but when the time is right, I will know.

I have always been fascinated by symbols. I think that the things we do in secret or with hidden meaning carry powerful messages to the Universe.

When my uncle Dick died, his ex-wife, Priscilla, asked me to see to it that a big flower arrangement was placed on his coffin. She phoned her instructions from Canada, and I knew there was more to her motive than a show of respect and bereavement. It was an act of defiance.

The flower arrangement on the coffin at his funeral became a powerful symbol. In spite of a cold, yet grieving family that despised her, here was a colourful token from an ex-wife who still loved my uncle and was heartbroken at his passing. The rest of the family was really pissed off. But such is the power of symbols.

I really liked Priscilla, and was sad when they divorced. I took the flower arrangement home and kept it until all the flowers had dried properly. Then I crushed them into a powder and performed a secret ceremony with Kay. We scattered the flowers at the church where Dick and Priscilla were married. That was a symbolic gesture of defiance and love. I know that while we performed this ritual, all of those who had gone before stood in the spirit world and smiled. We never told Priscilla what we did, but I do know that her spirit was with us in that small place. All was well.

* * *

Race registration in Rio took place at the Maracana Stadium. As we drove there, Silvia assumed the role of tour guide and proudly explained, "This is the largest stadium in the world. It was built in 1950 to host the fourth Soccer World Cup, with a capacity of over 200 000 screaming fans. Is pretty big, no?"

Silvia was right, the stadium was impressive. She went the extra mile; she showed me the players' dressing room. Then she walked me down the tunnel where so many great soccer stars had walked before. Silvia's enthusiasm for the game was more than infectious. She danced a samba, waving her arms as we walked.

"Hey, Tomas, imagine walking here with Pele or Ronaldo. Imagine the end of the tunnel. What must it be like to walk this short distance, and into the sunlight to the roar of a quarter of a million fans? This is what Brazil is all about."

We stepped out of the tunnel and found ourselves standing in the cavernous stadium, the pride of the nation. For a single moment I stood there and felt a sense of a life so exhilarating. I wonder if any of those soccer heroes ever tired of such an act, and I wonder how many were mindful of the hopes and dreams of 200 000 screaming fans. In this country the "beautiful game" and Brazil are one and the same thing.

Rio de Janeiro must rank as one of the most beautiful cities in the world. Back home I know that Cape Town has a matchless splendour, but it is difficult to draw comparisons. In similar ways it is difficult to draw comparisons between the beauty and splendour of different marathons. In Rio, there are the outstretched arms of the statue of Christ, Sugar Loaf Mountain and Rio's beaches, all in the sweep of a view that embraces a journey well made. Silvia took her job as tour guide seriously and once we finished with race registration at the stadium, she took me on a tour of the city.

She easily found parking at our first destination, St Benefice's Monastery. The buildings are over four hundred years old, and as I walked into a cavern heavily ornate with gold, I became aware of the strong influence of the Catholic Church in South America. Silvia went to one side, lit a candle and placed it in a holder, while I walked open-mouthed down the centre isle, staring at the rich and colourful arc of the high ceiling.

Basil, my father-in-law, would be at home here. There was such peace and tranquillity in this church. Strange, a familiar smell seems to permeate all historic places of worship. It is a mixture of incense, ancient buildings, burning candles and fervent prayer. Mindful of the spiritual nature of my quest, I sat in a pew and offered a prayer to the Christ hanging before me.

"Please let me not falter, be my strength on the road."

I opened my eyes and looked up, Silvia was sitting at my side.

"So Tomas, now we go to Corcovado, before the sun sets, you want to see the Christ statue — no?"

She was a careful and considerate driver, and took me the long way round, through a cool, leafy forest. The drive up the mountain had many twists and turns and each time we passed a walker or runner taking on the steep incline she would give a friendly hoot. "You think they are getting ready for the marathon?"

Presently we reached the base of the giant statue and parked in an empty bay right at the start of the stairs leading up to the Christ. Silvia didn't immediately bid me out of her car. Instead, she lit a cigarette and regarded me carefully, I felt the question coming.

"So Tomas, tell me. You must be a very rich man, no? That you travel around the world to run your marathons. She drew long and pleasurably on her cigarette and blew out a blue plume of smoke.

"No Silvia — not at all. I am not a wealthy man, and I do not have the time for wandering around the world looking for answers."

"Then why?"

God, I wish she wouldn't smoke.

"I believe that it is a poor reason to say that we do not have the time or the money to follow our dreams. We short-change our lives if we do not passionately do the things we are meant to do. But the sad thing is that we get distracted. Imagine meeting our Maker, and He or She asks: 'Well was that fun or what? What did you do with your life?'

"Will we have to look the Maker of the Universe in the eye, and say that we didn't do very much? Or say that we couldn't, you see, because we never had the money. Besides, there was work to do — and we just could never find the time for that Soul shit.

"This journey, to run a marathon on each continent, is more than just a dream. Dreams are sometimes things we hold only in our heads, speaking to us often only on a superficial level. What I am doing is more than a dream. I am going around the world with the deliberate intention of growing my Soul. This is a one-year investment in the growth of my

Soul. No matter how much money you spend on the growth of your Soul, it can never be enough. No matter how much time you spend, even a lifetime, it is not enough. I run my own one-man business and most often I struggle to make ends meet. But it is worth finding the resources for a journey such as this.

"I have given everything to my family. I don't often buy new clothes for myself and I don't own anything fancy. I have spent virtually all my earnings on educating my children, and on holidays.

"So this is the first time in my whole married life that I have spent time and a small measure of money on myself. On my Soul."

Silvia sat mesmerised as I blasted forth — again the drag on her cigarette and the blue plume of smoke.

"*Si*, Tomas I understand, you are a good man — so now come — I show you the biggest Christ in the whole world."

When I asked Silvia why it seemed so easy for her to get parking virtually anywhere she wanted, right at the door of every tourist attraction, she at first became thoughtful. I thought it was a fairly easy and innocuous question but I sensed there was pain in the answer. After some thought, she told me of her husband, Raimundo.

"He was a good man. A policeman."

We leaned on the railings high above the city. From the base of the statue on Corcovado we looked out over Copacabana, Ipanema and the Sugar Loaf. The city sounds were distant from up here.

Silvia lit another cigarette and continued, "One night he was called out to one of the favellas — squatter camps here in Rio, to break up a fight. He was shot and killed in the crossfire. I miss him very much. With Raimundo's pension payout I bought the taxi. Most of the security guards at Rio's tourist attractions were friends of Raimundo, all ex-policemen. They helped me in the difficult days just after his death; they supported me, not only with prayers and the burning of candles, but with money and food as well. So, I know most of these guys, and they keep me a parking place to honour the memory of my dead husband."

Silvia took me to the Museum of Contemporary Art in nearby Niteroi. She did so at my request — and I am happy that I pressed her into this. The museum is built like a flying saucer suspended on a pole. Its design is elegant and once you are inside this building, given the odd structure, the windows are at an interesting angle to the floor. With the waves coming in towards you, it almost feels as if you are flying toward the city over the sea.

As I looked out over the bay towards the city, I felt Silvia's presence. Unconsciously she held my hand and we stood in silence. There was an uncomplicated sensuality about her. She sensed it too, and squeezed my hand.

"Ah Tomas, your wife must be a very lucky woman, no?"

I wasn't sure how to respond, but standing there with the sweep of Rio before us, in each other's company was reassuring. I was not a silly old greying man; I was still attractive to women. How long would that last, I wondered?

"You know something, Tomas, your work is your art." The spell was broken, but the intimate conversation was not. "I was thinking about what you said about your soul."

"You take the work you do and you separate it from the money you make, yes? This is how you become prosperous. We should look at our work as a great artist views his paintings. When I drive my taxi, I see it as so. When I take you to the scenic places in Rio, it is my art — I do not do it as a job. Tomas, I am wealthy, I am the lucky one, and Raimundo taught me to think in such a way.

"If we work only for money and for reward we sell our soul to the highest bidder. We become a slave to someone else's purse strings. Many people think that to be rich is to have much money and many possessions. To have land and shares and even motorcars."

It is late afternoon and the sun catches the sea and it sparkles. The bridge over the bay between Niteroi and Rio is over ten kilometres long and we drive on a road surrounded by water.

Silvia continues: "I say that our true wealth is measured not by what we have, Tomas, but by how little we need. You take your wealth with you wherever you go. It is measured by what kind of artist you are. It is the peace and unity you feel for your family.

"Ai, my English is not so terrific, but am I making sense? It is the reputation that goes in front of you when you walk into a room, that is your wealth. It is your struggle. That is your wealth. Tomas, I read a book once called *The Prophet*. In that book it says, 'Work is love made visible'. I believe that."

Evening was closing in now and I was tired. I enjoyed this woman's company, but I wanted to be alone. Silvia turned into the Copacabana and looked directly at me. "So Tomas, Rio is beautiful, no? I will take you back to your hotel so that you can get some sleep. It is your big day tomorrow."

"Thank you for a wonderful day, *obrigado* Silvia." I kissed her on the cheek. She smiled and drove off.

Later that evening I sat alone over an early pasta and pondered the difficulty money presented in my life. It was always in the pit of my stomach, a feeling that stalked me in the small hours of the morning. I toss and turn before I go to sleep. It is a precious commodity that intrudes upon a soul weary of creditors and bank managers.

The art of having money is like any other craft. Money is no more than a commodity and it should always remain so. It is a way to unlock human potential and it can give wings to dreams.

Somehow the world has got it all wrong. Wayward football players and rock stars who set bad examples as parents, spouses and pillars of society have an unrealistically high value placed on them. Yet a teacher, charged with shaping the hearts and minds of our future leaders is paid a pittance. This is because the world does not fully understand the meaning of true wealth.

That is the problem with the world-view of money, and it is little wonder there is such poverty. Society places wealth on the wrong values. True value should be placed where it fully lies.

I understand the principle of training conservatively and with caution. I know that too much, too soon will result in injury. This principle must also apply to the creation of wealth. The principle of consistent, persistent training must also hold true in our quest for wealth.

* * *

Very early on in my quest, the lack of financial resources was keenly felt. Whether it was fate or good fortune, I will never know, but the gods smiled on me and blessed my mission. The letter came as a complete surprise. I had done some consulting work for an American bank. It was hardly a big deal, and I attended only two meetings. I was asked to submit a proposal. A week went by and I was asked to submit a tender. The proposal had suddenly become a tender. I was told that there were other parties competing for the same business. I sighed, rolled my eyes, and reluctantly complied.

A few months later I heard, via the grapevine, that someone else had been awarded the job. When I made enquiries, the sordid truth became known. The bank had actually awarded the contract two years previously, but consistent with their business practice, they were compelled to use a tender system. I was just filling in the numbers to suit corporate compliance.

I was outraged. Even more so because they had begun using all of my ideas. They had used me not just to fill in the numbers, but for my knowledge of local road running. I wrote a strongly worded letter to the chief executive. I was not expecting a reply, and was satisfied that getting it off my chest was sufficient satisfaction. But before I departed for my first marathon the letter arrived. More than the letter of apology, the cheque was generous. It was enough to take me halfway through this pilgrimage.

If I have learned anything about money, it is to trust in the abundance of the Universe. There is a generosity out there that is huge, and all it takes is a small measure of faith; but only a small measure.

* * *

This was going to be a marathon battle of epic proportions. The sky was clear and it was humid. Because the race was point-to-point, we were bussed to a place forty kilometres out of town. The starting time was set for nine in the morning. The temperature was already 30°C and it was getting warmer.

Nothing can repress the spirit of the Brazilian dawn. This *corioca* is an ethos of pride, sensuality and infectious enthusiasm. It is everywhere. Take this spirit and mix in a passion for football, and the start of the Rio Marathon resembled a Mardi Gras rather than a race. In every other race in the world, at the gun, you have to watch your footing around all the cans, bottles and debris left by a patiently waiting start crowd. But here the debris is kicked, dribbled and, for more than a kilometre into the race, skilfully kept in play and eventually kicked into touch.

Soon enough we settled into a pace. I wondered what the day would bring. The entire race is run along the beachfront. I had my doubts about the heat, though. Normally one gets an idea of how well an event is organised by the presentation of the first drinks table. This should be placed at the three-kilometre mark, and should have cold water and at least one other drink. By the time we ran past the six-kilometre mark, with no water in sight, I was beginning to get really worried.

The writing was on the wall. There was going to be little on the road by way of drinks, and it was going to be hot, humid and uncomfortable. But there is a maxim I use when coaching Comrades Marathon novices: "Make sure of your medal". That is what I intended to do.

The cut-off was six hours, so I had almost an hour longer than what I was used to. Slow down. With the oppressive heat, I needed to drink often, so wherever I could, I stopped at a garage or house, and begged water. I carried water with me on the run.

By the time I reached the halfway mark, the organiser's folly was evident. The runners were dropping like flies. Still, I chose to enjoy this run as much as I could. The thirty-kilometre mark was somewhere on Ipanema Beach and it was close to lunchtime. Runners had to dodge ice-cream carts, prams and people. Chaos, sheer chaos.

The blaring music at the finish could be heard at least three kilometres away. I ran along the shoreline with Sugar Loaf Mountain on the other side of the bay. Many yachts were out in the festive holiday atmosphere. I was home, and my medal was in the bag.

The final run-in was fine, and for the first time in almost the whole race there was a well-stocked water table with hardly a kilometre to go. I made it with only a couple of minutes to spare. This was a prized medal that epitomised the struggle.

Much later that evening, I sat in an open-air café enjoying the sea breeze. All the doubt and the fear I had had while in New Zealand was gone. I had only two more marathons to run. I could now see the end.

I looked across at a table close by. A couple was sitting there ignoring each other. She was attractive in the movie-star sense, and he had the air of a high-powered executive. The atmosphere around them was one of excruciating sadness. I called the waiter over. "What's their story?"

"They are a wealthy couple that own an apartment here on the Copacabana. They work in São Paulo and come here for weekends. She is having an affair."

The waiter filled my wineglass and continued, "She sometimes comes here on her own and meets a man without her husband.

"I think he is an investment banker and I think that she is on the radio. Do you know that it costs millions of dollars, US, to have an apartment here on the beachfront?"

Their sadness seeped into the fabric of the evening. Over the road there was a huge carnival going by. It was a "Gay Pride" march with over half a million participants. There were enormous floats and people in outrageous feathered costumes. The music drowned out this sad couple's despondency. The flow of life will wait for no one. No matter how sad and lost you may feel, the sun will always set in a magnificent blaze of glory.

"*Ola* — hey Tomas, I did not expect you to be here — how did your race go?"

"Hey Silvia — nice to see you — sit down and have a glass of wine with me ..."

Suddenly the air of sadness and despondency lifted — I sat on the Copacabana toasting my hard-fought victory with a new friend.

Wealth — now there is a difficult concept to really understand.

CHAPTER 9

Picking up the Pieces

———o0o———

The morning is grey and heavy. There is a wet chill in the wind. I run down a small incline over a rail bridge on this quiet Sunday morning. The university town of Grahamstown spreads out before me. It is the end of October, late spring, and the town is wearing its new green foliage. A fresh promise of the coming summer. The white church spires are set against a steely sky.

Old Jed is running at my side — he smiles wryly — "Who knows if this is good luck or bad luck?"

"Yes Jed, who knows?" We run on in silence.

Behind me on the rail bridge is a gap where the safety railing has been ripped out. The car had careened through it and launched into the air. Below, the electrified railway line, a wall and beyond the wall at least a thirty-metre drop. Then Mrs Witbooi's well-tilled spinach patch.

The car had twisted and turned in space, and after an eternity thumped backwards into the soft earth. The safety air bags exploded open in the twisted wreck. My eldest daughter was in the driver's seat, blood pouring from her nose, dazed and confused ...

"I want my Daddy ..."

I believe that all events are connected. Everything that takes place has a wider context and as we stand as actors on the stage of life, fate is the scriptwriter.

* * *

I was excited about my next marathon. It took a lot more planning than the rest, but the idea of running in Chicago was tantalising. I was making a detour via Nashville, which would be the highlight of my entire pilgrimage. Situated here was the sister Hospice of the one I work for in Krugersdorp. Because of my fund-raising efforts, I had been appointed to the Board. This visit would be the first official task in my capacity as the newly elected chairman of Hospice-in-the-West.

The opportunity to explain our home-based nursing programmes, describe our innovative ways of dealing with HIV/Aids locally, and of course extort money from wealthy, guilt-ridden Americans was something I was beginning to relish! As our currency weakened against the dollar, it seemed my job would be easy and pleasant. All I would have to do was make a well-prepared presentation. The American Hospice had arranged a room full of sympathetic people to see a pilgrim from Africa on a mission. I spent many hours on my training runs rehearsing my speech.

Then there were the South African friends I was going to stay with. This part of the American trip was going to be the most pleasant, productive and enjoyable of all my running so far. Washington was also on my itinerary. I had special running friends there, thanks to the Internet.

I was more than excited to meet with Mark, who was going to run the Chicago Marathon with me, and would be my host and tour-guide in America's capital. I trained Mark by email for over a year-and-a-half, and he came to South Africa to run the Comrades Marathon twice. When he was in Durban it gave me great pleasure to show him and his girlfriend a slice of South African life. Now it was his turn to reciprocate. Mark is loud, full of himself and has an enthusiasm that knows no boundaries — so typically American, so easy to like.

Every part of this North American trip took on some sort of special significance. Because of US President George Bush's renewed "War on Terror" after the 9/11 incident in 2001, the entry requirements to the US had become tedious and difficult. Obtaining a visa from United States Immigration meant hours of queuing, interviews, mounds of paper work, and even fingerprinting. I viewed this officialdom as a necessary part of my pilgrim journey. A part where I had to display patience and humility.

It was late in September that the symptoms first made themselves felt. Initially it was the familiar lethargy of flu. But by the next morning I knew that this was more than a head cold, and after a visit to the doctor and blood tests confirming that I had Hepatitis A, my visit to America was on hold.

"Tom, I know that you are feeling sick now," said a patient and sympathetic doctor. "But it is going to get a lot worse — I will phone you tomorrow and tell you what strain you've got, when we have done a complete analysis."

The doctor was right, I did get worse, a lot worse. Hepatitis A and its symptoms are not unlike a massive hangover. "You will feel like this for six to eight weeks and there is nothing you can take for it."

I did some reading and found to my disgust that you get Hepatitis A from infected human faeces. I shuddered at the thought and tried to think of how I could have contracted the illness.

"You will be surprised," said my soft-spoken doctor, "how many people in Johannesburg get hepatitis. It comes from all the finest restaurants in our leafy northern suburbs. Bet you eat a lot of salads, well ..."

Nothing happens by chance and this, too, happened for a reason. I had to believe that, because the alternative would send me into a spiral of despair and depression. As I pulled the blanket over my head and yearned for a swift death, I tried to reach into my tormented Soul and seek some sort of answer.

I had planned this pilgrimage for two years. I had been faithful and true and I had come so far. I had trained hard, and for the Chicago Marathon I was physically and mentally stronger than I had been for years. I had appointed a friend to help me raise money for Hospice. My book, temporarily on ice while I finished a big publishing project, was more than half written. Even that was taking on the shape of something publishable. My quest — my pilgrimage — was beginning to show progress and promise. I could even finish it.

Why then? Why did circumstances conspire to thwart my most earnest attempt? Why do bad things like this happen to good people like me? Now the sad truth lay before me. I could not reach my goal of running a marathon on each continent in the year I turned fifty.

I had to believe that this sickness had some significant spiritual import. All my sympathetic running friends, and all the reading I did, pointed squarely to one sad fact. Hepatitis is serious. Serious enough that you dare not do any strenuous exercise for six to eight months. There it was, my quest lay before me in tatters.

"What, Tom, what is your attitude?"

Life seemed to be begging an answer. In the first weekend of my illness I lost six kilograms and soon after that, not only did the whites of my eyes turn yellow, but my skin did too. I would wake up in the early hours of the morning drenched, and needed to change my pyjamas twice a night. The headaches were penetrating and the nausea stayed with me for days on end.

"What, Tom, what is your attitude?" Death, take me now.

During this time I became calm and clear. In a state where my body was as depleted as my mind, I felt no panic, no resentment; only an air of clarity and calmness. My spirit was reaching to me. My Soul was speaking to me, and in the stillness I heard it.

"Nothing happens by chance, this is a time of great spiritual growth." Life was saying to me. "Be still and listen. Meditate and go within, and be patient. Trust your life. All you ever wanted to know, all your answers lie within yourself — just be aware."

I understood that I could find great meaning in this illness, if only I began to look. My physical quest was temporarily on hold, but now I was on a deep spiritual quest. This was an unexpected, but welcome journey.

* * *

I get angry, panicky, even scared when the telephone rings in the small hours of the morning. As it did the day my mother died. All the more so when it is over the weekend. This can only mean trouble if your daughters are out. "Good morning Sir — how are you?" This is an oddity in the New South Africa. Perhaps it is part of public relations training, but at two-thirty in the morning, to phone someone up and enquire about their health is pushing the boundary of PR to absurd limits.

Do I launch forth and explain how my hepatitis is giving me bad headaches and that I am losing weight? Or do I blast the man for intruding on my restful space? Discretion, Tom. Discretion.

"I'm fine thanks, how are you?"

"Oh, I am fine thank you. My name is Constable Mabulatsi and I am phoning from the Grahamstown Police Station."

My mind begins to race.

"Are you Mister Cottrell?"

"Yes.

"There has been a motorcar accident and a man will phone you shortly."

My mind is screaming. I am in free-fall panic mode. The phone goes dead; an eternity is the time it takes for the phone to ring again.

"Hi, my name is Gavin, and firstly let me tell you that your daughter Megan is fine. I am at the scene of the accident and my son Mark is fine as well. The car, my car is a complete wreck."

Gavin did not sound fine, he sounded in shock.

That early Saturday morning was punctuated by phone calls from Gavin, the police and doctors at the hospital. All assured us that Megan was fine. Then, mercifully, a groggy, familiar voice came to the phone and assured me that all was well — well, okayish.

"Hello, Daddy?"

I breathed out slowly. Megan told me she was in shock, in pain, but that she was alive.

Someone had to get down to see her soon. It looked like the one who would have to go to Grahamstown and sort out this mess was me. Kay was in the middle of setting school tests and it would be almost impossible for her to leave her teaching post right then. So, hepatitis or not, I prepared to go to Grahamstown.

The journey to the airport and the flight to Port Elizabeth was a stern test of my resolve. I was still ill and much of the transit jostle was a sickly blur. I was unsteady on my feet and I had a constant pounding headache. Still, I was needed. Megan and her friend Kelly met me at the airport. Megan was on crutches, and as I hugged her she sobbed.

"It's okay, Daddy's here."

The time I spent with Megan was special. We worked together, arranging for her year-end exams to be extended into the New Year. Together we made appointments to see unsympathetic professors who showed resounding indifference. I bumbled about in a hepatitis daze, and she hopped about on crutches, trying to get the hang of negotiating the thousands of stairs that make up the Rhodes campus. Most people were helpful, but for both of us the process was tedious.

I could sense Megan's spirit was low, and momentarily I caught a glimpse of her as she struggled to come to terms with her accident. She looked vulnerable, hurt, sad. She might be an adult, but she was still my baby.

Once all the business at the university was done, I paid a visit to the doctor to get a report of her injuries and a copy of her X-rays. Then I asked Megan to take me to the site of the accident. At first she was reluctant. But eventually she took me there, to the rail bridge.

I stood looking down and I went cold. The hundreds of things that could have gone wrong were all too stark. The drop was more than the height of a double-storey house. The flight path of the car was over a railway line with electric cables overhead. There was a solid wall separating the final resting place of the car from the railway line. With so many things that could have gone wrong, I looked for the one thing that had gone right. The angels must have been with her on that fateful night.

Just as I was after my accident fifteen years before, my daughter was lucky to be alive. We stood there arm-in-arm as the rain came down. It was cold and the afternoon wore a melancholy gloom. I knew we were both lucky survivors, but I was tired, sick and I suddenly felt very old.

"Come, let's go to Kenton-on-Sea and sit on the beach."

The drive to Kenton was shrouded in my own thoughts and in mist. Cold, despondent, we sat together on the beach, huddled against the wind. And then it happened. There was a moment of sheer magic as we gazed out to sea.

It became clear to Megan what she would make of her year ahead. She knew what she wanted to do. "Opportunity" was the word she used as she became excited at her prospects of finishing her degree. She also wanted to do an honours degree. The path ahead suddenly seemed clear to her and the gloom of the afternoon lifted. Not all was lost; she and I came away from the ordeal with both understanding and wisdom.

* * *

"So tell me Tom, what do you make of all of this? Do you finish now that you have been ill?" It was Terry, mic in hand, blinking — ever penetrating, always probing.

"Tell me Terry, did you watch the Olympic Marathon on TV?"

"I'm a sports writer, following a pilgrim on a marathon run. I would not miss the Olympic Marathon for anything."

"Well, the favourite to win the women's race was Britain's Paula Radcliffe. There was so much riding on this race for her. It was more than money, more than national pride, this was the making of Paula Radcliffe herself. For her, I believe it became an all-consuming obsession to win the Olympic Medal.

"She took the lead early on in the race as she always does. 'She does not know how to run from behind — she only knows how to lead,' said the British commentator.

"The Chinese girls running around her knew this only too well and they played her. They ran her into the ground. By the time she hit the thirty-seven-kilometre mark, her race was over, she was spent, completely exhausted. She sat on the side of the road and wept.

"Terry, she baled the race with less than five kilometres to go. So pathetic was she that journalists back home were calling any quitter, any loser, anyone who threw in the towel a 'Paula'. Terry, I am no Paula Radcliffe. Not in this instance. I know I am down right now, but I am not out. The show goes on."

If you cannot run — walk
If you cannot walk — stand
If you cannot stand — sit
But don't wobble
And if you might wobble ...
At least close your eyes ...

It comes down to picking up the pieces of a shattered dream. The progress of a pilgrim is blocked by ill health. Blocked also by the loss of momentum and even the loss of interest one feels when lethargic and depressed. Megan's accident brought home all my fears, of her mortality, and my own.

The Olympic Motto — *Citius, Altius, Fortius* — Swifter, Higher, Stronger.

"The important thing in the Olympic Games is not to win but to take part, just as the important thing in life is not the triumph but the struggle. The essential thing is not to have conquered but to have fought well." These are the words of Pierre de Coubertin, founder of the modern Olympics in 1896.

How do I emerge from this with victory? I had to look to the ideas I understood best. Instinctively I knew the answer has to be found within the context of a marathon run. Where better place to go than the 2004 Men's Olympic Marathon?

The young Brazilian — Vanderlei de Lima — made a brave, perhaps foolish break early on in the Athens race. This was the Olympic Marathon, and it is usually taken as a tactical, slow run. No one expects great times, but everyone expects a race of tactical skill, more like a game of chess. Lima made a bold move early on in the game. His opponents gathered in a pack behind him and were slowly sizing him up.

The Brazilian runner was out front for a long time, too long. For lonely and cold blows the wind for the leader. But he settled into a workmanlike pace and began to think of the Olympic Gold Medal. Behind him others were working hard to catch up, and the Italian Baldini looked every bit a contender. But the race was not over yet. It was in the final stretches of the race with only six kilometres to go that disaster struck.

For Vanderlei de Lima the biggest challenge of the race, of his marathon career, and perhaps the biggest challenge of his life came in the form of a demented former Irish priest, Cornelius Horan, who darted from the roadside crowd and tackled the Brazilian to the ground. It happened so fast and surprised everyone. Lima was on the ground, Baldini was closing in, as was Keflezighi, the American marathon athlete.

For many, when disaster strikes, there is a moment of truth. There comes a time in every calamity, a moment of clarity, and a sense of reckoning. Time stands still and at its source there is nothing but truth. Many recognise this moment when their lives are forever changed. It is the point where there is no going back. For young Vanderlei de Lima, this was such a moment.

The sounds blocked from his mind, the crowded blur of an Athens street left him with only one decision — one destiny — get up and run. Slowly at first, confused and a bit dazed, the young athlete began to run, struggling to find his pace, looking deep within himself for composure.

The defining moment came when the Brazilian ran on to finish his race. Baldini ran past to claim gold and Meb Keflezighi took silver, but the standing ovation went to Lima.

With a big smile on his face, blowing kisses to an adoring crowd, Vanderlei de Lima finished his race to claim the bronze medal. This was surely one of the most heroic moments in athletics history.

The Olympic Committee believed that this singular act was worthy of recognition, and the highest and most revered award — the Pierre de Coubertin medal — was bestowed on Lima for his exceptional demonstration of fair play and Olympic values that day.

* * *

In a hepatitis daze, I stand with my arm around the shoulders of Megan. She is on crutches but alive. If there is any emotion I wish to express, it is gratitude. I know her spirit is strong and she will pick up the pieces. Her race will not end like Paula's. Together we hobble off the beach and back to the car. We will never quit.

My work in Grahamstown was done for the moment and I prepared for the flight home. Before leaving I went for a light jog, to the accident site. Rain and cold. As I stood there, it was Jed who joined me.

"She is alive and I am grateful, this is good luck."

Jed looked down at the spinach patch, and then at me. I knew what his answer would be.

I had a long road of recovery ahead. When could I train properly again? I was unsure. I knew that North America was going to have to wait as I tried to regroup. But I was not a quitter, and my resolve at this point was strong. With small, hesitant steps at first, then breaking into a light jog, I worked on my recovery. Before long I got back on the road. It was a great struggle at times, but my eyes were firmly fixed on Hong Kong in February 2005.

There are no real answers as to why things happen to us in the way they do. The world is an unfair place. Often we have no choice, no control over our fate. Life is a series of seemingly random events, and we bob on a tempestuous sea at the mercy of the elements. The only control that we have over our fate is the choice of our attitude and our mind-set. In this grain of truth there is great hope. But I also know that nothing happens by chance. For me this is the great reconcilable paradox of my journey.

I am glad of that incident in a crowded Athens street. I am pleased a demented Irishman tackled a Brazilian athlete to the ground, for in this tableau I have had much to reflect on. In it there is much truth.

"Come Tom — Hong Kong is waiting."

The spirit of Vanderlei de Lima is calling to me. Sluggishly I tie up my running shoes and sigh. Thankfully it is summer and it is light outside.

"Who knows if this is good luck or if this is bad luck?"

CHAPTER 10

Asia

The development of our spirit

——o0o——

My lungs are bursting, my heart is pounding, and I am bent double. I have just pressed the button on my stopwatch and I am too tired to even look. But I know it is in the bag. Yup. 36:14. Not bad, a week ago I was struggling to break forty minutes for a seven-kilometre time trial. I am drenched with sweat, but I am happy. Everything is on track. I have been running against the clock for over a month now. I have no option if I want to bring home a medal from Hong Kong.

Anton is a running mate who will join Kay and me in Hong Kong. He is also planning to run the marathon. He does business in the Far East and he pointed out the one scary rule about the upcoming race. The cut-off time: five hours.

Five hours! I have not run a marathon in under five hours

for over two years. How the hell am I going to do this? Anton also pointed out how long hepatitis hangs around and messes with your running. Like an unwanted drunk relative at a wedding reception. I feel weak. But I am committed to my pilgrimage. I am determined to come home with the medal.

If you want to run faster, then you have to run faster. That is the plain and simple truth about running. Shorter and faster. The training philosophy comes from Olympic hero Emil Zatopek. "When I was young, I was too slow. I thought, why should I practise running slow? I already know how to run slow. I must learn to run a hundred metres very fast. People said 'Emil, you are crazy, you are training be a sprinter. You have no chance.' I said 'Yes, but if I run one hundred metres twenty times, that is two kilometres and that is no longer a sprint'."

In Helsinki in 1952, Zatopek won the 5 000m, 10 000m and the marathon. In all three races he set new Olympic records. For speed work he became my mentor.

I dropped the long Sunday training runs and went back to racing. The final build-up to Hong Kong was a twenty-mile race in Springs. An old running partner, Derek, joined me. "You are wasting a lot of time at the drinks tables, I reckon you can save a least five minutes if you drink on the run," he said.

Derek was right, and I needed all the help I could get, every minute I could find. This race was going to be touch and go. Under five hours, God, this was a huge challenge.

* * *

The room is dark — I breathe in and I breathe out. Fiddle about ... Two ... Three — ah shit it's gone again ... I breathe in, and I breathe out ... One ... centre the mind ... Two ... keep the focus — keep the focus on a central point at my "Third Eye" ... Three ... I gently push away all thoughts of the mundane and counting my breaths is the only point of focus and ... Four ... I am calm now, I am breathing, and for the next breath ... Five ... I have done it ... I have focused on a point in my mind — almost a physical point — I have done it for five breaths and I have cleared my head of all daily thoughts. This is the beginning of my meditation, now I am ready to make myself one with the Universe.

I make time to meditate. Each meditation is different. Like prayer, it is personal and individual. No right or wrong. There is a strong connection between mind, body and spirit. I have felt its strength while running.

I breathe ... I count and I focus ... relax and get my mind and body and spirit to focus ... I am relaxed but alert, I am aware of my surroundings ... I am ready.

As I sit, I reach out and try to find my spirits. Those I touch beyond this life. I greet my family and friends who have moved on. I reach out for their vibration. I become aware of my mother, a strong and warming influence. I wish I could have experienced more of her during her lifetime. I become aware of my grandmother, steady as a rock. She was a woman of humility in her lifetime. In death this elevated her to great spiritual wisdom.

I become aware of this wisdom. I know that when one of such calm and resolute watchfulness is with me, I am well looked after. There are others, Risto, killed in the accident with me. He brings an energy and also a feeling of forgiveness. He taught me forgiveness. I feel the presence of Sally, different now, calming and loving. And so the room fills with the dear departed, and almost like a great family gathering we chat and enjoy fellowship.

This is only the first step, and soon I must leave and move on to the next spiritual plain. I bid them farewell and move to a quieter spot in my mind, where I am aware of only one entity. My Teacher.

This spiritual Guide has watched over me since before my birth. In my imagination he is Eastern, perhaps Chinese, and my name for him is Sen. I enter his presence and respectfully bow in greeting. He is equally respectful as he greets me. I am aware that I am in the presence of great calm and wisdom. I pause here with Sen, while he instructs me. Sometimes it is about business, sometimes family or something unrelated.

Sen's attitude is always one of kindly love and deep concern. I sit and listen and Sen instructs. I believe that my deeper insights, and my life's understanding comes from this source. When I have finished with this second stage, I move on. With great reverence I bid my Guide farewell and move on to the next level.

At the third level there is a different vibration, for here the angels exist. These entities are not concerned with the day-to-day functions of material life. They are more concerned with my spiritual progression. In my mind this is the realm of angelic existence. It is a good place to stop, pause and feel the calmness. The detached transcendence over all troubles. It is said that if you wait a hundred years every decision will be right. In this place of angelic calm, there are entities who have watched over my growth for more than a thousand years.

They watched when as hunter-gatherers we ritualistically buried our dead in the Ice Ages. They know our ancient wisdom and our early understanding of worlds beyond. These angelic entities were with us when we created civilisations in Egypt and in Greece. It is they who look over us now, with understanding and a deep and abiding love. I sit in the presence of my Guardian Angels.

When I feel completely calm, loved and fully understood, it is time for me to bid these entities farewell, and to move to the fourth and final level. Here I enter the "Light".

I find myself in the presence of all the Prophets, Sages and Saviours. I place myself in the very presence of God. This brings inner bliss. I bathe in the warmth and the light that emanates from God. I feel the love that transcends our human understanding. This is a moment of pure happiness and bliss. I thank God for life and for light in my life. I feel grateful that I am aware of such depths.

There is something inside of me that is ancient. Deathless. That knows about life, birth and survival. All the deep questions that need answers are met there. That ancient part of me is my "Totem". My Soul. It has lived for more than a thousand years and is the wise, strong part of me that is beyond death. In my meditation I see it as an ancient statue of solid granite. Polished but not smooth. It stands high; a powerful and silent witness that has lived many lives.

I have lived here for many lifetimes. I have been a man and a woman. A soldier and a mother. I have known the burden of great wealth and title, and I have been a slave. I have died in childbirth and I have been stillborn. I have been many races and creeds. I have hunted on the plains of Africa, and begged in the streets of Constantinople. All this I carry within. I am here and now, as an extension of this journey of discovery.

My meditation is now complete and I am aware of the surroundings of the room. It is quiet. It is dark, just before daybreak. Breathe in ... One ... Two.

I turn to the assembly before me and greet each with respect and with love. I bid my Soul good day. I thank my ancestors for the time I have had with them. I go to Sen and bow with reverence, and promise to be more disciplined. I go to my angels and stand before them and absorb their love and council, and then I stand before God. I feel the light and the warmth. I feel the hand of God on my heart and on my mind and on my life, and I give thanks.

Breathe out and ... Five ... the sun has not come up yet, but I am calm and happy. In the distance, the call of a hadedah. I have spent an important part of my day getting ready ... I know this will be a special day.

* * *

Anton came to our hotel one evening and invited us to meet a close friend, Sampson, who lived in Hong Kong. He was a wealthy businessman from nearby Mong Kok, and we had dinner at his office. Anton explained that this was not an unusual practice; many Chinese do it.

"They work damn hard, long hours," he said as we stepped out of the spotless underground station and walked along a street alive with traders, music and people hurrying home.

Gaudy neon lights flickered and danced on the buildings. Above us, on the corner, was a huge screen advertising hi-fi equipment. It lit up the whole street. "It is easier to have your meal at work and then go home," Anton continued as we went through the complex customs and pleasantries that make up Chinese etiquette.

Later that night Sampson took us to a lookout point on Hong Kong Island. "This is probably the most valuable piece of real estate in the world." Below us were the lights of the city, and beyond lay the bay and Kowloon. Five hours. How the hell was I going to run in under five hours?

* * *

Zen and the art of making a fire.

I can feel winter coming. The icy cold front comes in from the south, blown over the steely grey Atlantic. As I look southwards, I can feel my own depression at hand. It is not that cold yet, but the primordial animal instinct inside can sense its coming. It will be cold tonight. The unseen front is approaching. I sense that my life will change. No longer the summer days of outdoors. Most of the trees have lost their leaves and they take on the look of death. In their stark branches you can see the abandoned birds' nests, once summer lodgings for a family now gone.

I bend down and in my mind I complain of the thankless task of making a fire. It is a harsh thing to be taken for granted. There is no gratitude for a fire-making man. While I busy myself with these thoughts, I become aware of someone standing close by, watching. I glance to the left and slightly behind me, and there is Sen. "I have been sent here to teach you to make a fire."

He is dressed in his ceremonial dress.

"But I already know how to make a fire."

Sen is quiet, and we regard each other. In my mind I grapple with the difference between reality and this seemingly real individual standing there.

"Yes you do, but I have come to teach you anyway."

Then, "What are you doing?" asked my Teacher.

"I am making a fire," I answered. He stood over me, glaring. I knew from the scowl on his face that I had not given the right answer.

Angrily now, "What are you doing?" He had with him a long ceremonial sword. When he barked out the question a second time, I saw his hand grip the handle. I had clearly given the wrong answer. I watched him.

This was not going to be easy. Surely if this strange man was sent to be a teacher, there had to be some Zen in our discourse. I see what I see. I am what I am, and I do what I do. Could it be any simpler than that? What am I doing? A simple, yet profound question.

I stood up to face him. He was about my height, perhaps a little taller. He was thin and wiry. I hoped that my slow movement and the deliberate avoidance of eye contact was non-threatening enough. I knew this could be a turning point. My mind was racing, what am I doing? Whatever my next answer was to be, I had to give it with the utmost thought, and judging by his demeanour, it had to be given with a great deal of respect.

"I am warming this cold house for myself and my family, Master."

Sen seemed to relax a little, he loosened his grip on his sword, and I thought I even saw a smile flicker in his Oriental eyes, so dark and mysterious. "Good, that was a good answer for a young student, but I can see that you have much to learn. To begin with, better you warm your house for your family first, and then yourself. Get the order of things right."

Whatever we do, no matter how simple, every action has profound meaning. Our task is to develop clear and ongoing mindfulness of these simple tasks. Each time I busied myself with the anthracite heater, Sen would appear and the lessons would begin. One night the fire went out, and by morning it was cold. I would start the fire again in the evening, after the day's work. As evening fell, and the weak sun sank, creating cold shadows across my life, I stood at the anthracite stove and pondered.

Sen made his presence felt. "Open the top of the stove and dig out all the unused coal." I recognised the lesson immediately. The only way to get started on any job was to roll up my sleeves. I had no choice but to get my hands dirty.

As I dug the unburnt coal out of the stove, I wondered how many of us don't want to get our hands dirty. We would prefer to stand in front of a dead stove wishing it was cleaned out. We wish someone else would come along and clean out the stove. Many of life's tasks are just so. Rearing children, keeping house, and even running a business requires us to get in and dirty our hands. We need to pull out all the debris first. We need to clean out the mess. Painstaking but necessary work.

Now to build a new fire. Sen stood at my side. He looked approvingly at my hands, now black with the task of unloading and loading the stove. "What do you understand?"

I thought deeply about my dirty hands. About how we remain spectators. How we observe life from an "impassionate" distance, and are hardly affected. This makes us less than human. Take the poverty of Africa. How impartial are the wealthy to the cries of starvation? The rich do not want to put their hands into the stove and get them dirty.

The beggar on the street dies and the body is removed. A woman holds her baby, both are crying, the baby hungry, the mother desperate. There is more than enough food and comfort for all, but not for these two. We read the next morning about a baby found dead in a dustbin. Shaking our heads, we think how awful this is. It was the same woman we passed in the street on our way back from lunch yesterday. The same one who asks us every day for money, food, anything. The same one we ignore every day. Ah, but what can we do? There will always be the poor and the needy. They must help themselves.

I argue passionately and raise a finger. It is dirty and black. Sen looks on and there is a faint smile. "Go on," he says.

Many people are afraid to love. Better not to be hurt than to have loved for one day. We fear getting our emotional hands dirty. In fear, we crawl into the sun for what warmth it may offer. The emotional hurt of rejection makes us stand on the sidelines with our hands folded, hoping someone else will take charge. We cannot be involved in saving the world. But it is our own stove that we must dig into and clean. It is an act of life.

"Good," said Sen. "Reflect on this and apply the lesson."

The spirit and attitude we bring to our stove is important. The stove must be cleaned, but we must go beyond. Sen taught of the "perfect fire". For the house to have proper warmth, the flames must be so hot that they are blue. For the house to be warmed in time for the family meal, this has to be done by five o'clock in the evening, as the winter sun sets. The stove must be full and a full bucket of anthracite ready at the side for the morning. All of the ash must be gathered and the plinth properly cleaned.

Sen was patient with his teachings. "Seek perfection in performing a simple ritual and you will accomplish many of life's seemingly complex tasks. A perfect fire is not a once-in-a-winter's-night achievement. You shall have to do this task daily. You must think of your most perfect fire each day and perform the tasks to achieve this.

"This," said Sen kindly, "is the very essence of duty. More than this, your family will take it for granted when you perform these tasks for them. You will have to do this without expecting gratitude. You will be admonished if the fire goes out and the house grows cold. Your reward is your service. It is only in the doing that you will find your joy. Do this and you will find your innermost peace and your freedom. Remember the lesson of the fire."

* * *

I stand at the window of our hotel room. Over the road is Kowloon Park and the street below is Nathan Road, the start of the marathon. Since two o'clock this morning there has been activity, and now small groups of runners stand huddled around any available shelter, out of the morning drizzle. The barriers are erected and the starting banner is stretched across the road.

In the park I can see people moving slowly in Tai-Chi style. In spite of Western influences in Hong Kong, there are a great many Chinese traditions, and in the early morning mist, there are many practising one form of martial art or another. There are also people sitting in meditation.

"How am I going to get through this with my dignity intact?" The question was for Kay. She was in the bathroom and could not hear me.

I became aware of Sen standing next to me. "I shall teach you about your marathon." Slowly he pulled his ceremonial sword from the scabbard and with a fearsome cry he took a swipe at me as if to behead me. Dazed at this sudden change of attitude and surprised at his fluid movement and speed, I simply froze and stared at him. Our eyes met.

"Focus. That is what will get you through this race. Focus." I have watched you train for this and you make a good warrior-student. You wanted speed as your ally and you learned to run fast. That was focus. I know about your leg and how it hurts. I also know how sick you were before this race, but this is the time to focus. If you want to achieve here in Hong Kong, you must focus. If this sword were merely a stick, it would not behead the enemy. But it is a deadly weapon in my hand."

Sen stood back and assumed a Samurai attacking stance, ready to strike. "Watch the sword, and avoid the blow." He swung hard, I ducked, but maintained eye contact. "Good, warrior-student, you will do well in Hong Kong."

Anton was in a jovial mood as he joined Kay and me for a light breakfast. I had a slice of toast with honey, washing it down with a cup of strong coffee. Great planning this was, we stepped out of the hotel foyer and onto the starting line.

"Good luck, hey Tom," Anton shook my hand.

"Good luck, love, see you at the end."

Kay kissed me and she and Anton pushed their way forward to the faster runners. I was unsure of the outcome today, but I knew I had a few things on my side. I was reasonably well trained for this. I knew I was also lighter and faster than for any other race on my pilgrimage. Add to that a cool, overcast day. All the elements that could make up a good, fast race were there. Now it was up to me.

As I stood at the start I saw Sen in the crowd. Our eyes met and he bowed. We never lost eye contact. In Buddhist style, I put my hands together and bowed back. Focus. It started to drizzle lightly. The gun went.

The first watering point was in Tsim Sha Tsui. I followed Derek's advice: drink on the run. I got through the first five kilometres, checked my watch. I had not raced like this since my accident fifteen years before. It was exhilarating.

Most of the race was on the highway. We ran out of Kowloon and into the New Territories. It was starting to rain hard when I reached the Cheung Tsing Tunnel. The sheltered protection of the tunnel was a welcome respite from the cold driving rain. By the time I ran out the other side, the rain had relented, but it was still cool; uncomfortably cool.

The climb up to the turning point on the Tsing Ma Bridge was strenuous. Then I saw her, Kay was running past me in the opposite direction. She looked surprised. Part of the marathon is out-and-back, so the runners still going out can see those coming back. I knew that the turning point was not far ahead. I was not that far behind Kay. I looked at my watch as I ran past another watering table. Nice and comfortably on time, I could break five hours, but there was still a long way to go.

The bridge is high above the bay and the mist was rolling in. While running back through the tunnel and the New Territories, I felt a sharp stab in my ankle. A reminder of my limitations. Besides the bridge, this race was scenically sterile. It was highway, punctuated by a few single spectators. In many respects I was glad of this, for it gave me the space I needed to focus on my watch, the marker boards and the pain.

Running back, Kowloon was ahead, beyond that the Western Harbour Crossing. The rain had stopped and I could see the tall buildings on Hong Kong Island, shrouded in mist. I was slowing down, battling with the pain. The moment of truth came when we left Kowloon and ran under the sea for about three kilometres. The tunnel was womb-like. Suddenly there was no wind or rain. The orange glow of the lights gave a surreal, detached feeling to the race. The kilometre mark ahead was the thirty-fifth, and although I had slowed down, I was still well on track.

The power and the fury of Sen, sword drawn, took me by surprise. He stood at the marker board and screamed "Focus!" Such power, such strength. I was unstoppable. I responded and screamed back: "Focus!" The tunnel echoed.

I came out of the warmth and onto the busy, noisy streets of Hong Kong Island. Sen met me with the same ferocity at each remaining marker board. At marker forty-one, I looked at my watch for the first time in five kilometres. Kay had finished and was standing with Anton. They were shouting and waving at the end. Sen was there too, our eyes met and we bowed in deep respect. "Well done warrior-student."

I crossed the finish line with both fists clenched in a victory salute. I flung my head back and with all the strength I could muster I yelled out from deep within my Soul, "Focus!" The clock was stopped at 4:51:37, almost twenty minutes faster than any race on this pilgrimage run.

* * *

"And where are you going?"

We had no idea. Bangkok was a very different experience to Hong Kong. We stopped off there for a few days on our way home. Hong Kong was orderly, clean and disciplined. Here, things were chaotic, hot and noisy. The little man was trying to help. We wanted to go to Jim Thompson's House. The famous landmark museum of an American who revived Thailand's silk trade.

The map we were struggling with showed us that the house was only two blocks away. We were going to walk. But our problems started when we realised the street names were in Thai, and bore no resemblance to the English names on our map.

"And how are you going to get there?" he asked.

"We are going to walk"

This man was getting irritating. "Well it may take you about two hours from here."

Bullshit, I thought. It's only two blocks away.

I think he was reading my mind, "You may think it's two blocks away, but look at these streets."

They were jam-packed with all sorts of traders, clothes and food.

"It is also very hot."

No shit. It was at least 39°C.

"There is another way, you could take a tuk-tuk."

Almost on cue, one arrived next to us.

"And how much do think you will pay? Not two hundred bhat, but fifty bhat." I could see the set-up coming a country mile away.

"If you did walk to Jim Thompson's you would be disappointed. Do you know why?" This conversation was becoming comical. "Well, I'll tell you, you will have to wait for an hour, it only opens at twelve o'clock."

He then launched into a spiel about his king's reign. "And how long has Queen Elizabeth been on the throne? I'll tell you. Fifty-five years, and our king? Our king has been on the throne for sixty years. And do you know what?" Ah puleese.

He set me up for a handmade suit at one of Bangkok's finest tailors. I hardly ever wear a suit, but given the price, and the expert and cunning sting, it is an incident I cherish. Later that day Kay and I were walking back from Jim Thompson's.

"And where are you going?"

"Just bugger off, I already have a suit."

That evening Kay and I were enjoying a welcome cold beer in the hippie area of Khao San Road. We sat on a balcony high up above the street.

"I think I am beginning to understand what you are doing on your pilgrimage, I really admire you." One of Kay's greatest compliments.

The plane home left at midnight. I checked my watch. It was my birthday. I was fifty-one. Officially this pilgrimage was over, now I was in injury time, but I had a doctor's certificate.

A few days later, at home, I was teaching some of my students about living and motivation. One student gave me a gift, a music CD he had made in honour of my runs on each continent. It was beautifully packaged, and much of the music carefully chosen, but one thing in particular caught my eye. On the inside cover, underneath the song titles, was a picture of an unsheathed samurai sword next to its scabbard. I saw this and caught my breath. I looked across at Willem, my student, and our eyes met. He smiled and bowed slightly. The message was clear. Focus!

CHAPTER 11

North America

The care we take for our community

——o0o——

I saw him sitting on a bench overlooking a tranquil lake in Central Park. New York had hardly begun to stir. Out on the lake, water birds were making a din as they chased each other and scooted over the surface.

The buildings on each side of the park were still in shadow, but in the chill of first light, it would not be long before the sun bathed this scene with golden warmth. On the path behind me a few solitary runners were out. They seemed a far less friendly crowd than my fellows back home. All so wrapped up in their own little worlds, headphones on, faces in neutral.

"Morning!" I yell.

Silence.

"Fine thanks, and you?"

Stony silence.

Lame Deer is a Sioux medicine man. "You are on time, this is good. Now we smoke pipe and we talk." "But I don't smoke," I wanted to protest. I thought better of it. With reverence I took the offered pipe with both hands and drew in.

"They tell me that you pick up three stones from each land you visit."

"Yes I do."

"This is a mistake."

"Oh?"

"The number that is the most *wakan*, the most sacred, is four. This is the first teaching. There are four quarters of this earth. There are four winds that blow across our prairie. There are four seasons and four basic colours."

With a sweep of his arm across the arc of the buildings on the other side of the lake, Lame Deer continued, "This universe is made up of four elements: earth, water, fire and wind. There are four virtues that a man should possess. We Sioux do everything by fours. When you take your stones from our land, you must take four."

"This is not a good thing," I protested. "For then I lose the symmetry of things, I only have three stones from each of the other lands. I will have to go back to each and find another stone."

The sun had broken through the surrounding buildings. On the lake the light danced and sparkled. Lame Deer drew deeply on the pipe, and the sacred smoke billowed all around us. "There is no symmetry in most of life, it is we who need to make it so. To find your missing stones from all the other lands is a task for the future. Our work here is never done, it is always unfinished."

"Hey old man, are you going to just sit on that bench staring into space all day, or are we going to finish this run?" Kay was behaving like a playful child.

* * *

The morning was cold. I had driven for two hours to get to this healing sanctuary in the mountains. It was difficult to find, and to compound matters the directions I had been given were not accurate. The building was hidden behind an unkempt hedge. The walls were rough stonework. I stepped through the door into the gloom and looked around. There were pictures of spiritual guides on the walls. Beyond, there was another room. I heard someone stir. I knocked.

Lame Deer was a renowned healer. People would drive for many miles to visit him to seek spiritual guidance and healing.

"Come, come in. I am glad to see you"

We embraced. I was the apprentice and I wanted to learn more about the art of healing. He would have me sit and meditate, and quietly watch as he performed healing rituals on the sick. Every now and then, he would invite me to place my hands on a patient. Quietly humming, with his eyes closed, he would invoke the Great Spirit to this place to bring healing.

On one visit, he taught me how to breathe. "We think it is water that is important for life. We think it is the food we eat that sustains us. Well, it is not. We are able to go without for days, more than a week even. It is the air that we breathe that is the most fundamental force of all life. Learn how to breathe, learn about life."

Lame Deer stood with his feet apart, as though rooting himself to the ground. "This is what you must do to breathe properly. First empty out your lungs, so that your body holds no breath. Then, with power, breathe in."

I watched as this great man drew in a breath. It came from the very bottom of his being. His face looked typically Sioux as he heaved in a huge gulp of air and his chest swelled. It seemed to take forever. Then silence. His eyes were closed.

He exhaled with a great roar. "When you breathe in, draw in from the very soles of your feet. Breathe in the spirits of the earth. Feel the whisper of the prairie. Breathe in the secret knowledge of the bobcat. There is great and ancient wisdom in the earth. Breathe from there."

All of the healing power that I have comes from the earth. It comes from the Great Spirit. When I breathe in, I get my magic from those secret places and it gives me my power.

* * *

The training for Nashville was near the end of the road, the last marathon — well almost the last. There was still Antarctica, but I'll talk about that later. I was tired. I had been running and training for marathons for almost two years and I was beginning to get stale. Yet I still loved getting up and running every morning. My life had changed. Running was more a lifestyle now, so I felt quite at home on these chilly autumn mornings. On many a training run I would fantasise about the North American leg and what it would be like to run the last mile of the last marathon.

Terry goes over his notes and dives right in. "Tom, this is going to be your last marathon. What about the seventh continent, Antarctica?"

"Terry, this is *my* pilgrimage and as such I get to make up the rules. To my mind what makes a continent is as follows: there must have been civil commotion, a war, bad government, or a good measure of corruption before you can define a land-mass as a continent. In the case of Antarctica there has been none of the above, so to me it is not a continent."

Terry is unsatisfied. "But you have not done it all until you have done Antarctica."

"True, Terry, but for now this is where it ends and the icy land-mass will remain part of my unfinished business."

"But ...?"

"I have a plan, Terry. I'll talk to you later."

The last of my bath water runs out.

* * *

The view from the Empire State Building puts the whole of the "Big Apple" into perspective. Despite the cold, I am happy to be here showing Kay what little I know of New York. A mini honeymoon for us. A good time for adventure. During the weeks before we left for the States we had been bickering like two old hens in a coop.

It's a time to rediscover the child in us both. Seemingly more important things have crowded out that playful creature over the years. I stand behind her and point out the general direction of Forty-second Street. "There Kay, there. Times Square. Let's go and have supper there."

In the overwhelming gaudy neon shock that is Times Square, we took photographs, strutted around and shopped. There was Bubba Gump's, a theme restaurant styled on the movie *Forrest Gump*. I took this as a sign from heaven. Any running pilgrimage to the North American continent would be incomplete if we did not dine here, in the restaurant of the ultimate distance runner.

Our waiter was an out-of-work Broadway singer. After the meal and too much wine, I asked him to sing. We sat hypnotised as he sang *New York, New York*. Now that deserved a good tip. As Kay and I staggered the three blocks back to our hotel, she reminded me we could have fed a small African country for a month on the tip I gave.

"Yeah, and I haven't even got the CD to show for it."

We were both in exuberant spirits; the chill of the evening, the frenetic New York buzz, the effects of a long flight, and the wine. It was all that, I know. Kay and I howled with hysterical laughter, two children in a park sharing a joke where neither of us knew the punch line. Reason, be damned. This was pure unadulterated passion, and we howled into the night. It was just so good to be like two little children, a special moment for us both.

* * *

Before me on the table lay an ammunition box. It was brightly painted with Africa's "Big Five", coloured with patterns in typical African style. My task was to explain to an attentive American Hospice audience what it represented. Later I would present it as a gift to Alive Hospice in Nashville.

I wanted to use this opportunity well. This was our sister Hospice, and fate had a hand in my presence here. I had missed the Chicago Marathon in 2004, but as the gods would have it, there was a marathon right here in Nashville. I was able to fly two kites on one string. Run, and see how a first-world Hospice operated.

"This box used to contain ammunition," I explained. "The caregivers at Hospice use them because they are waterproof." What I was holding up was a "memory box". I knew in this cool, well-ordered establishment, I had to tell my story well. This place was so far removed from the trauma that was Africa's, and I wanted to be properly understood. I stood on the podium and looked out into the crowd. I saw Lame Deer standing at the back.

"Be with me, Great Spirit."

A big part of our South African Hospice programme is looking after Aids orphans. Into a memory box such as this we put the personal memorabilia of dying parents and we give it to the children who are left behind. An audiotape or CD of conversations with their parents. Voices kept for a lifetime. Photographs and a Bible or Koran. Wedding rings and other small personal items are carefully and reverently placed here for children to later remember their mothers and their fathers.

As I went through my presentation, picture after picture was shown of the work we do in Kagiso. Many I had taken myself, only a week before.

"We do not fully understand the numbers that make up the Aids problem." I showed graphs of the shift in patient statistics and how Aids was becoming more prevalent in our own Hospice. I asked a Nashville nurse how many patients he cared for on average. "I am really stressed at the moment because we are understaffed, I have twelve patients at the moment. But normally I have ten."

I rolled my eyes and thought of our nurses, angels of mercy in Kagiso. Each has a minimum of forty-five patients at any time. How the hell do they cope?

Lame Deer stood with his arms folded at the back of the auditorium. I paused and took a mouthful of water.

"Now I will explain why I undertook this journey in the first place."

Much earlier, in South Africa, I had felt the presence of Lame Deer at a Hospice camp for Aids orphans. It was a warm and pleasant spring evening and the air was sweet. Dinner was over and we were sitting around a campfire. The moon had just risen above the Magaliesberg mountains. It was full and it bathed the gathering in soft silvery light. Each child had a *jembe* drum and they were drumming out a complicated and subtle African beat around the fire.

Lame Deer, unseen to the children, was dancing medicine-man style amongst them, and our eyes caught. "These are your children, this is your future. You must look after them."

"Haiya, haiya."

"Cherish ones such as these, they belong to you," Lame Deer was emphatic. He was directly pointing to me. I know he is right.

"Haiya, haiya."

"Your deep love comes from all who are around you. Cherish your people, be of service to your community."

* * *

I hated Country Music. Until I ran the Nashville Country Music Marathon. In typical American style, this race was a huge commercial venture. The good news about such blatant and outright monetary intent is an outstanding level of organisation. Right from the time I entered, a regular stream of emails enticed me to buy all sorts of memorabilia. Then there was the well-appointed Expo, held in a huge downtown convention centre. Outside of the London Marathon, this was the biggest event I had run on my whole pilgrimage.

Before the race, Kay and I visited the Nashville Museum of Country Music. Running in Country Music's heartland, you either have to yield to its melody, or be swamped forever in the ample bosom of Dolly Parton. As we walked around on the "audio" tour, the history of the music unfolded. I am ashamed to admit it, but I came away with a new appreciation for Country Music, and even bought some CDs. The best exhibit in the whole museum was a gold car owned by Elvis Presley. In all of Nashville, that had to be the clincher.

On a drizzly, unseasonably cool spring morning, the sixteen-thousand throng was out to have a party. It was a race of festive proportions. The music belted out, the upbeat man on the mic at the start knew how to whip up the crowd's enthusiasm. I was in an expansive mood to enjoy my ride down marathon avenue in the king's limo. Oh Yeah.

For large parts of the initial stages, the running was an out-and-back affair. The effect was running against a steady stream of competitors coming the other way. Pumped by the incessant beat that filled every corner of the race, I ran close to the centre of the road and stuck out my hand. The oncoming traffic was quick to catch on, and in no time, I had many a good mile of new friends and well-wishers. High fives and "howdys". "Good job" was the slogan, good job indeed. The insular, aloof runner that was New York was transformed into an exuberant and friendly citizen of Tennessee.

The energy emanating from those thousands was electrifying. The opening magical miles carried me well into the "dead zone" of the race. When I got into the dreaded place of fatigue and pain, there was yet another band pumping out volumes of energetic music, yet another crowd dancing and singing in the streets. Nashville has vast tracts of parkland and country estates, so this race was more than just an action-packed Country Music concert; it was beautiful as well. The support at the side of the road was enthusiastic, sometimes even hysterical.

The stadium and the finish line was still a good distance yet, but in all of this excitement, I gradually became mindful that my long journey was coming to an end. This would be the culmination of almost two years of planning and training. Take your time, live the moment. "Be here now," is what I told myself.

This, in all likelihood, was going to be my last marathon. Ever. After twenty years of distance running, with well over a hundred marathons run and five Comrades Marathon medals, it was time for pause and thought.

The last mile. There it was. The last mile of the last marathon. Accomplishment. This was a long run. I had come a long way since the first steps taken after turning fifty. Kay had already finished the race and she jogged back to meet me. We ran together to the point where only finishing athletes were allowed.

"Well done, see you on the flip-side."

The music had been belting almost the whole way.

"And here comes Tom Cottrell, all the way from South Africa." Obviously picked up my details from my race number.

As I turned the last corner a sea of South African flags in the finish corridor greeted me. The Nashville Alive Hospice team was out in full force. And they gave me a real "Southern Comfort" welcome. I hugged them, kissed them and spent a while at the side of the race just breathing in the atmosphere. There had been many moments of utter bliss on this pilgrimage. This was just such a moment. I felt truly alive.

With only a few hundred metres to go, I charged off to the finish, fuelled by adrenalin, love, Country Music and a sense of madness. Ahead of me was a runner sprinting for the finish. I drew level and pulled back a little. I gave him a side-ways glance. He thought I was trying to out-kick him to the finish. He sprinted — I matched him. I grabbed his hand and smiled.

"Oh, now I got ya man, good job."

We finished together holding hands aloft. That day I finished a hero in 5:23:17. Good job.

The Five Hour Pilgrim is at the end of his quest.

* * *

This pilgrimage stands all too stark, like the trees stripped bare in winter. The goal I set for myself will never be achieved. That is the sad truth. I wanted to run a marathon on each continent in the year I turned fifty. Even though I still have the doctor's certificate on file, stating I was not to run last October due to Hepatitis A, on my own terms, I failed. When I finished in Nashville I was nearly sixty days too late.

I wanted to tell the story of this quest by the time I turned fifty-one. But, more than three months after my birthday, I am still scribbling notes and patching up badly written chapters. I wanted to raise a million rand for Hospice-in-the-West. To this day, I have no idea how much money I raised; I only know that it is way off the mark.

Could this whole pilgrimage be written off as a monumental waste of both time and money? I may as well write my whole journey off as the demented quest of a middle-aged madman. Ultimately, this *was* the philosophical meanderings of a nobody.

With all my heart I know that this is a limited view. I know that our lives are not made up of destinations alone. Life is not made up of impossible goals set before us. There is much more to it than that. I don't underestimate the value of the destinations set forth in our lives. They are important and give positive impetus to reach our ideals. It is important to be one hundred percent committed to these goals.

On a much deeper level I know that our real strength, our depth comes from the journey we travel. It is how well we make the trip. I may have "failed" on all three counts, but that has become irrelevant. During a period of a year, I set out on a daunting journey. Now at the end of the pilgrimage I find within my life a richness and interest that has changed everything. In distance running, the race often does not go to the swiftest. Rather, it belongs to the athlete who just keeps running.

To ensure that I would remain serious, I told everybody about my quest. I started with my family and then I preyed on my friends. Soon, complete strangers were told of my unbelievable pilgrimage. My reasoning was simple. If I ever ducked out, I was to become the laughing stock of everyone I had ever told. The stakes of pride were incredibly high. I wrote down my goals too. I was public and vocal. My commitment was all-embracing; it was total.

Tell me the time a race was run in. Was a record set? Then this I know for sure: it will fall. Set the bar as high as the world record; someone will break it. Rather than speed, give me the heart of the runner. Hand to me the character of the athlete, the mind and the will. What makes up the training session and how the race is approached is of far more use to a pilgrim than a record that is sure to fall.

Roger Bannister stood on Iffley Road track in Oxford on May 6, 1954, about to attempt to run the world's first four-minute mile. If he succeeded, he knew he would make history. There were a few who believed it possible, but at the time the four-minute mile was, for middle-distance runners, a dream, a goal, a destination.

Later, "we shared a place where no man had yet ventured — secure for all time, however fast men might run miles in future. We had done it where we wanted, when we wanted, how we wanted ... In the wonderful joy, my pain was forgotten."

These were the reflections of the journey one man made in breaking through a barrier self imposed. In today's race, the athlete comes last who cannot break the four-minute barrier. It was Bannister's journey of self-belief that sets the pace today.

So it is with my own journey. Physical, mental and spiritual growth has been mine. This growth is far more important than any self-imposed destination, now unreached. I did not choose a mid-life crisis of destruction. The milestone of my passing age did not pass unnoticed. Rather, I stepped onto the road and became a participant, not an indifferent bystander with arms folded. That is the essence of my journey.

Lame Deer watches the thoughts flit through my mind like late geese taking to the sky. He waves and leaves.

What of the critic who points out the destinations not reached? What of those who tell us that our best is not good enough? I say the critic is a coward. Would such as one of these ever step into the arena, ever enter the race? Better to be a fallen hero, one with blood and dust on my face. Better that than to be the distant, aloof and cold critic. The critic will never journey, never understand passion.

The shoes I have run in are beginning to look particularly road-beaten. They have endured heat, and they have endured rain. For them to be allowed into New Zealand, they even had to endure the customs official's washing machine. They have their own familiar smell, but these are the shoes of a runner. I recall the empty and lonely room that was my mother's flat, when I held a pair of her unworn shoes to my chest, and made a pledge, so long ago. The shoes that have carried me so far have been worn; they became the shoes of a participant. I held nothing back.

I must remember to ask dear old Terry next bath time about critical bystanders and passionate participants. Meanwhile the last continent waits, for a different run.

CHAPTER 12

Antarctica

Unfinished business

———o0o———

The medal could be made of ice.

I see it before me like no other medal I have ever seen. Pale blue with a solid brass date bar "2006". A work of art. It sports a bronze border, square with rounded corners.

It's made of glass and in the centre is a frosted relief map of the entire continent. Substantial. A small and yet subtle feature is the use of bronze inlay. A small emperor penguin — a creature so symbolic of the continent — is etched clearly on the bottom right corner.

The gold looks splendid. The silver medal's etchings disappear into the glass, making them difficult to see. The cut-off for silver is four hours, and I am glad that I would be too slow for that. But the bronze medal, with the dramatic contrast of colour against the glass is the most beautiful of

153

them all. The cut-off for the race is eight hours. I feel my chances are more than reasonable.

Normally I am not hung-up on medals, but when I saw this one, I knew that I had to make it to Antarctica.

Scott Seaward is a man incapable of completing a sentence when under pressure — and he swears a lot.

"What the fuck ..."

"What is going ..."

I first came across Screaming Scott when I worked on a TV programme for the Comrades Marathon. Scott is a legend and is respected as the best sports producer in South Africa, probably even the world. He looks the part too: long scraggly hair, a wild salt-and-pepper beard. He always wears a jersey no matter what the weather. The big ill-fitting affair completes the look of madman explorer.

Not many know that he is a frustrated amateur Antarctica explorer. He has been to the Southern Continent on several occasions and has attempted to walk, unaided, to the Pole. On three attempts he has almost made it, but it still remains an ambition of this loveable, explosive and expansive man.

When I told him of my plan to run a marathon on each continent he regarded me with a scorn that I found surprising.

"I don't suppose ..." he really didn't have to finish the sentence — I could do that for him.

I knew he would ask me if Antarctica was included in my itinerary. I also knew that I would tell him "no" and he would launch forth, if not in the most articulate way, on why any journey, spiritual or not, would be incomplete without a run in Antarctica.

Screaming Scott was mad, he was passionate, and he was buying the drinks. By the time we had drunk too much and dawn was breaking, the thought of running on the Southern

Continent seemed so logical that I phoned a panicky Kay to tell her I was fine and that I was going to run the Antarctica Marathon.

The Internet took care of details and dates. Before I knew it I was corresponding with Randy Hawton, correspondent and chairman of the "Seven Continents Club", in Colorado. As the emails began to get serious, it seemed that with Randy, all things would be possible.

February would be a good month for the run; it would be summer time. You don't want to do this in the winter, trust me pal. I trusted Randy. I would fit this in before my fifty-second birthday. If I could do this, then ... then ... I could do the whole lot. Seven continents. A tantalising thought. A dream. Scott would come with me as a running partner. It was all falling into place.

The problem, the big problem, was money. If I went, and it was a big "if" ... it was going to cost me big time. The costs in dollar terms looked scary. Translated, it amounted to almost a hundred thousand rand. It was time to talk to my family because the stakes were getting high.

Kay was philosophical about the whole thing. Her attitude was an interesting amalgam of resignation and resentment. Deep down she supported me, but when under fire and duress her inner anger boiled over in frequent arguments. Slowly but surely, the royal queen of the household was becoming less and less amused.

In the end she agreed to place her sacred, if reluctant, blessing on the project. I could go on the strict proviso that I would continue to nurture, love and educate our daughters. And that both would have more than a decent send-off at a gala twenty-first birthday function.

A hundred thousand rand was more than twice the amount spent on the pilgrimage thus far. The journey to Antarctica would involve flights to São Paulo, Buenos Aires and then on to Ushuaia. Add to this a boat trip across the Drake Passage, this trip was going to require more than an ordinary budget. The stakes were high and the bank balance low. Clearly, the time to focus on things of this world was pressing — the earthly reality of unpaid bills and grocery packets.

Seaward was unperturbed. He was divorced with no real family commitments to speak of, so for him this was a great adventure.

It was clear. If I went on this journey I was stretching Kay's goodwill to breaking point. It was a very selfish act. Kay's gentle yet penetrating reality sat on the back of a logical argument, but a spiritual tug of compelling proportions called me to the quest. I sat on an isthmus of passion and reason. One hundred thousand rand was before me. Dear God, I could pay off a huge slice of my bond with that kind of money. In the end it was my decision. What agony.

* * *

"Well let me tell you, Terry, I think it is a very lame excuse not to follow your dreams. Lack of money and lack of time are not good excuses. How often do we put our lives on hold because we don't have the time or the money to follow what is true within us?"

"I see then you have made your mind up to go, Tom?"

"Yes Terry, I have — not an easy decision. Kay uses it in a lot of the arguments we are having, and believe you me we are having lots at the moment. But I came back to all the reasons why I am going on this pilgrimage in the first place. I think of the growth of my Soul, I think of the lessons I am learning, and I think of the person I am becoming, and I believe that in the long run this quest is a worthy one. So Terry — I am going."

* * *

I had done this before, the flight from Johannesburg, a stopover in Cape Town and on to São Paulo. From there, the connecting flight to Buenos Aires, where I spent an in-transit day in Argentina's capital. The city tour focused on Eva Peron's life. In the banking district we stopped at the Casa Rosado, or Pink Palace, where Evita (and Madonna) addressed the crowd in the Plaza de Mayo. Mario, my guide for the day, pointed out the solid-looking banks.

"There is no money, but at least we have the buildings."

The Casa Rosado contains the president's offices and is freshly painted on the side facing the square. "Perhaps the next president will have the money to paint the other three sides." Mario's laconic comment.

A three-hour flight down the Atlantic coast from Buenos Aires to Ushuaia. This "port at the end of the world" is on the Beagle Channel in Tierra del Fuego. It is a small town which does surprisingly well from tourism. Its port is deep enough for luxury liners and both the "Marco Polo" and the "Amsterdam" were berthed during my stay.

My ship, by far a more modest affair, was waiting for me at one end of the harbour. The "Professor Multanovsky", a Russian icebreaker, had been converted to carry fifty passengers. It would be my home for the next ten days.

Screaming Scott Seaward was already on board, and as I walked up the gangplank he was as enthusiastic and as exuberant as ever. He grabbed me and hugged me, "Good to see you, *broe* — I knew you would do this one."

My travelling companions were from ten different countries, including a honeymoon couple from Norway, and we ranged in age from thirty-five to seventy-five. The two passions that bound us all together were seeing Antarctica and our desire to run a marathon in unusual, pristine surroundings.

Kapitan Sergey Nestorov and his Russian crew of twenty-three were most unlike the types we had read about before the 1994 elections, thanks to censorship. These guys were friendly, professional and enjoyed rock music.

Nestorov was approachable, knowledgeable and in complete control of his ship. He welcomed us onto the bridge and into the chart-room, and painstakingly explained the intricacies of navigation. Especially the difficulties of crossing the thousand kilometres of ocean, the Drake Passage, that separates South America from the Antarctic Peninsula. The seas here have the reputation of being the most treacherous on the planet.

It was here that I discovered that I did not possess the sea legs of the well-salted crew. The passengers, mostly landlubbers, capitulated almost to the man (and green bride). The motions of the ship and the excellent cuisine provided by our Russian chef proved almost too much for even the hardiest marathon runners. But, after two days, we were beginning to get the hang of the rolling ocean.

On the evening of the second day came an announcement from the bridge. The sighting of our first iceberg. A tabular berg, five kilometres to starboard, about a kilometre long and fifty metres high. Holding the railing of the ship I felt awe as we gazed out to sea.

As we headed further south, we encountered hundreds of icebergs, but the memory of the first shall forever be special. At times, cruising those waters was like cloud gazing. We picked our way south, past colonies of penguins solemnly standing in groups on pack ice. In clear water we saw the ghostly depths of the submerged bergs. The water reflected greens, blues and even pinks of many subtle shades.

On day six we reached Antarctica, and we stepped onto the continent for the first time. We spent the night at Vernadsky, an Ukranian research centre.

This was the furthest south we would go, and where the marathon would be run. At latitude 65 degrees, it was just over a degree short of the Antarctic Circle. The nights were less than two hours long and were nothing more than twilight merging into pre-dawn. The stars were never visible.

We rose at seven the next morning for the race. Outside it was −40°C. On a late February morning in 2006, forty-eight of us waddled onto a bus with caterpillar tracks and were transported to the start. For safety and logistical reasons, the race was a two-lapper of twenty-one kilometres. The field was small but the back-up team was large. No Country Music here to carry us along.

The race started with the cleanest, bluest sky I have ever seen. I was aware of the enormous privilege it was to be here, run here. Cold beyond measure. I was aware of the sacrifices made by my family. I felt the tears well up in my eyes.

Scott sidled up to me. "Fuck, it's fucking cold — good luck."

He gave me a huge thumbs-up and the gun went.

The first five kilometres of this race were slow at best. We were all bundled up against the cold. As we warmed up we discarded our clothing and running became a little easier.

By the time I passed the fifteen-kilometre mark, I was running freely and quite happily, but I was right at the back. I had lost most of the cumbersome outer layers and was into a good and steady pace. True, it took me two hours forty-five to get to this point, but at this pace, given nothing untoward, I should make it in about seven hours forty-five minutes. Make the cut-off, get the medal and become a member of the "Seven Continents Club". What a way to finish my seven continent quest.

* * *

The men crouched behind the reinforced metal door of the landing craft as it made its way up to the beach. At first the small boat was out of the range of the machine-gun nests on the beachhead. The soldiers could see the spray of bullets, a hundred yards ahead. Soon they would be in range and in the sights of the Germans. The door dropped. The men were exposed to the ferocity of the fire. Many died on the beach.

This is the opening scene of *Saving Private Ryan*. Apparently the making of the movie was so traumatic for the actors that many of them had to go for counselling during production.

My demise on the Antarctic wasteland was equally as dramatic and equally as traumatic. Almost in slow motion, I felt the sharp pain and then the darkness. I remember falling to the ground and my head hitting the hard road, and I remember the taste of blood in my mouth and then the blackness. And the whiteness.

Scott sat before me, he was dressed in white in the whiteness of the barren Antarctic wilderness.

"What happened?"

"You fell. You never made the race."

Failure, emptiness — I had spent the family's fortune — I came this far and I shall return empty handed. I looked out into the whiteness and felt immense sadness and loss.

"Fucking hell, the missus will only be pissed off."

Thanks Scott.

How does one feel when the hopes of a mother or father rests on your shoulders, and you fail? What happens to those who don't — cannot — live up to the dreams of an expectant spouse? Where does one hide when an expectant nation wants you to win, and you don't? Where are the failures, the second placings, the nobody's. Bring them to me, for they are my children. Let them sup with me, for they are family.

* * *

"Terry, you have asked what happens if I don't reach my goals on this pilgrimage."

Terry sips his coffee, takes a long drag on his cigarette and nods.

"Well, let me tell you I have succeeded anyway. That I thought about this quest, planned it, and went down the road, is enough. So I set about running a marathon on each continent — I made six. I have a T-shirt from the London Marathon. It puts the odds of finishing a marathon, any marathon, at seventy percent. I know the odds of finishing the Comrades are higher, but South Africans are a different breed of runner.

"If you take seventy as the percentage of normal success, then to finish two marathons there is a forty-nine percent chance. Take this to six marathons and there is an eighty-eight percent chance of failure, statistically speaking. Terry these are serious numbers, and even at six done, I have beaten the odds — what do you think?"

Terry's head whirls at my figures.

"If I didn't raise the million rand for Hospice, no matter. I didn't just have a few beers with my mates, get a bit pissed and roll over. No way. I put my cock on the block. The world is just a little bit better because I was here. If I do not finish my book and it remains a pile of handwritten notes — I still came this far. I put my thoughts on paper and for one brief, magnificent moment I pretended to be a famous author working on a book that would not only express my love for my daughters, but would make some difference to the world."

* * *

Scott's eyes are the eyes of age. He has lines, smile lines that underscore his open, effervescent nature.

"What now?"

I think of some of the Hospice patients I have counselled. The subject of unfinished business is always present in the house of the dying. I am now in this house, and I look to Scott for my answer.

If the lesson is too great for this life, then may we return in another. If I have not enough experiences now, may the womb that bears me to the next life give me the experiences I need.

My life force is made up of the four elements: earth, water, fire and wind. I see the partial face of Lame Deer.

"Good," he says, "you were paying attention."

Earth elements have erected and solidified my bones and my bodily structure. It is the blood that courses through my veins and the fluids that lubricate my function. It makes me like water. There is warmth — no, heat — a fire that keeps my body in perpetual motion, and it is my breath, the very subtle winds. It is these rhythms and tides that sustain my life.

When I die, each element will collapse in on the next and I will become one with the white void in which I lie now. One with Antarctica. My body shall turn weak, and the earth elements will collapse into the water. As I leak and perspire, so the heat of my person will grow cold and eventually become the icy chill that is death. So my wind shall give out and I shall be no more.

Scott looks at me, unblinking — Well, Tom?

In any life some tasks remain unfinished ...

Icebergs are dangerous when the air temperature is below zero, as it is in the Drake Passage, even in summer. They melt from the bottom where the water temperature is above freezing point. After a while this causes instability in the iceberg. This mass of ice spontaneously and spectacularly overturns.

Where does my life begin and where does it end?

The "Professor Multanovsky" slipped its moorings and the pristine white beauty of Antarctica began to look like a dream fading into the wakefulness of day. I stood at the stern of the icebreaker and wept.

I was the only one leaving these shores without a medal. I had the long journey home. We left Scott behind to prepare for another assault on an unaided walk to the pole. He was waving frantically and shouted across the rapidly growing space between us. "Say hello to your fucking wife — great woman — you asshole."

Here where no war was fought, here where there is no government and few men have set foot. If my business with this world is unfinished — let it be in a place such as this. Scott, I shall return here to complete my quest, here in this pristine whiteness my task is unfinished, I will return. If not in this life, certainly in another.

I heard a crash in the sea to my left. An iceberg had turned over and the sea about it was boiling. I see Scott in the mist, but I am aware of something more now.

"Wake up Tom, it's time to get up."

Kay is shaking me. I blink and look up at the ceiling. Hell, where was I? Kay leans over and kisses me.

"Kay, you will not believe the dream I have just had."

CHAPTER 13

Rivers, Medals and Stones

——o0o——

There is a stream that runs close to the bottom of my garden. Often I have walked along its banks, unconscious that it was even there. Absorbed in my thoughts, dreams and fears, I did not even notice the water rushing by.

The word "pilgrimage" has affected the way I see and respond to the world. My quest is to express the mental, physical and spiritual impact of this sacred journey.

In miles run, I have almost been around the world. Like Tennyson's Ulysses "I am a part of all that I have met". I have met my Soul in unexpected places. Battled with sickness and disappointment. Battled physically on the road. I have exposed my insecurities in my writing. Yet I rejoice and celebrate my humanity. Now I tell you my story as an artist, that you may run at my pace, feel my joy and exuberance, understand my fear, and walk next to the garden stream with me.

In my imagination I enter the waters and am swept along,

a leaf with no control of my fate or my fortune. I am dragged along as the brook becomes stream and then river.

I lie on my back in the warm water. The current drags me downstream. It is as mighty as the Orange River, cutting its way through the Richtersveld — a desolate stretch of Namib Desert. I look up at the blue sky, I am pulled by currents. I muse about my life.

The power of the current is unstoppable. The force of life's current is unrelenting. Is it time? Is it events? Is it space? Is it perhaps all of these?

Just like the river, if I want to change direction, I must apply myself. Yes, I can go upstream, I can go to the riverbank — this is possible, but I need to paddle hard and work to achieve such a destination. Inevitably, the force of the river will hold sway. Surrender is a choice. I may be able, in short measure, to hold back the ageing process, but eventually I must surrender. I also may want to change my status of wealth and position. I can, with effort, do this, but the question will remain: will the pull of life's currents prove too powerful, and all such striving, will it come to naught?

Surrender. That does not mean I am helpless and without hope in the river. I still have the choice of sinking or swimming. I can choose the course down the rapids. I may choose not to smash myself on the rocks. I may out of sheer curiosity and exuberance choose to shoot a rapid. Surrender does not leave me impotent. Rather it helps me to better cope with the power and flow of something beyond my control. Ultimately we all will be washed out to the greater sea. Pushed into a vastness, abundant in life and variety. We will plumb greater depths. In the meantime, we must learn the ways of the river, and surrender to its flow.

I stand at the bottom of the garden. The water runs over the rocks and creates swirls and pools on its way to becoming a river. In its foam it struggles with itself. It watches my own frustrations. The stream crashes over rocks and debris as it understands struggle and unfulfilled dreams. In the turbulence, the water becomes muddied. Its struggle to remain clear becomes mine.

In winter, even when the chill and the drought almost stilled its flow, the knowledge and wisdom of the river was always there. It knew of my despair. All the leaves of the trees on its banks had fallen, and in the frost of an icy morning, all its potency and strength was reduced to an icy trickle.

My spirit, like the waters, has waited on the distant peal of thunder and the faint winking of lightning on the southern horizon. Where rain clouds gather.

* * *

Somewhere along my journey it was Christmas. Our family made the annual trek to Kei-Mouth. The town, if one could call it that, consists of a run-down public hall, a general dealer and a bottle store.

There in this backwater is "The Greeks", a restaurant and clothing shop. Eclectic, it is African in nature, and yet it could be in Brazil or on the Mediterranean. The décor and the Latin melodies wafting through the humidity make it an informal, comfortable place with Greek flair. Here I asked myself once again about the wisdom of a guide and mentor. What is it you want to learn from a mentor?

"Hi, mind if I sit down?"

I looked up. A runner, perhaps. I am so bad with names, not much better with faces.

"Hi, sure, sit." I did mind, I had come here for some peace and quiet, and I wanted to think.

"So?" he said.

"So what?" I asked.

"You called for me and here I am."

"I did? Who are you then?"

"I am your Soul. Can I have some of your coffee?"

Soon enough I had paid the bill and we were walking along a vast expanse of Wild Coast beach. The tide was out. We were alone.

"So what do you want?"

"I want to know what it feels like to be a loving God. I want to have that much love inside of me and I want to give it to my daughters and to my wife."

"And have you been able to do this?" asked Soul. I pondered this, I didn't have a complete answer yet.

"When I run, I want to feel my own strength and I want to test my own mortal and spiritual resources. I want to rejoice in my own physical being."

Soul skimmed a stone on the surface of the lagoon. It made five jumps. Pretty good, I thought.

"When I contribute through my Hospice work, I want to heal the wounds of pain. I want the dying to die in comfort with the knowledge of God's mercy. I want to heal my larger self. I have only begun to climb the mountain, I have only started the race."

My Soul placed his hand on my shoulder. "Remember when you were training a group of novices to run a marathon? You used to make them run to the top of a hill and you made them look back at their effort. On the early morning recovery run you would get them to review their race. You made them recall their mistakes; you would tend their wounds and build on their mistakes for the next epic run. Do you remember this? Well now it is your Soul that guides you. I have been your mentor on this journey, even before you were born."

Further up the lagoon a pont is slowly moving into the river. There are two four-by-fours on board and its deck is crowded with fishermen and their rods.

"All the knowledge, all the wisdom and all the teaching

you have ever received, I have given to you. Be gentle on yourself. I have watched as you allowed life to flow over you and steer you in its direction."

Far out to sea, almost on the horizon, is a ship.

"I have been your mentor since the running of the tides. Since your sun rose. I was with you when the dark clouds covered its light and when the storm broke. I am with you in the mellow light of this afternoon. So now open your eyes, listen with your heart. The race ends many miles from here and we have barely begun."

I stand in the shallow water of the lagoon, alone. All around me the water swirls. Deep in thought, I do not notice the tide has turned.

* * *

I find myself in a dimly lit restaurant. The Nelson's Eye is done out in typical English pub style and the proprietor is everything a pub-owner should be, friendly, warm and interested. Outside is a cold and blustery Cape Town, and the glass of red wine at my side gives me a special warm and friendly glow.

I feel sad that this journey is over. I am almost done living with the pretence of sitting in restaurants such as this, an accomplished author, working on an opus that will transform the world. I am winding down the letters, appeals, and begging from friends for my Hospice cause.

"Mind if I sit down?"

I look up from the page I am writing. It is my Soul again.

He takes off his overcoat, hangs it up and takes a sip from my wine glass.

"So Tom, your marathons are run. Well done old son — you and I have come a long way since you were forty-nine. You set out to grow us and look at us today. I want to take you back to the start of this journey. See the mountain you have climbed.

"Remember when you conceived this plan? You told everybody. What doubts you had! People looked at you disbelieving, even sympathetically. How mad they all thought you were, how misguided. Remember telling Kay and your girls your off-the-wall fifty-year birthday plan. Look at yourself two years ago.

"Go back and remember the state of your Soul then. How fearful it was, how small it seemed. How were you ever going to find the money? The time?

"You sometimes dismiss yourself as a demented middle-aged fart. Yet you recognise the importance of engaging the Soul, growing and nurturing it. This is one of life's most important tasks, many do not see it as such, and they cannot be bothered."

He takes a longer sip of my wine. I ask for another bottle.

"I want to take you back to that first marathon — the Buffalo in East London. It was your birthday, and Kay was running the race with you. You were so mindful of your first step. A magical race. And now you are here. Go beyond — it is not over."

I look across at my Soul. We have lived consciously with each other for over two years. I know this is the start of many other journeys, in this life and the next.

* * *

I have always felt that there were teachings behind many of the teachings of the great Masters. As a pilgrim I have tried to practise a measure of mindfulness.

A certain melancholy always sets in when a great challenge reaches its end. I recognised this when I finished my first Comrades Marathon twenty years ago, in 1986. For almost two years, my whole life had been focused on one small medal with a black and yellow ribbon. With every step I took in those days, with every mouthful of food, I would ask the question. "What would Bruce Fordyce do?" When the pain subsided and I returned to work to rejoin the ranks of mortals, my focus was gone. The early morning runs and the build-up was over. There was just another medal on a mantelpiece.

I understand there is a certain magic and uniqueness in first times. The second time I ran Comrades, it was not the heady challenge of uncharted waters. The first time carried unparalleled excitement.

I stand in my office. The sun is just coming up, and in the distance, the familiar, strident cry of a hadedah. Such an African sound. Unconsciously, I turn over a stone on my bookcase and feel its weight. I recollect where I picked it up.

When someone asked me how much money I put into this, I was a little surprised. I had no idea. I set off on this pilgrimage with no budget and little idea of how I would pay for it. Now that it is all over, I do not feel out of pocket or poorer. Besides, measurement in such earthy and material terms is irrelevant. And what do I have to show for it?

Nineteen stones and six medals.

The Buffalo Marathon medal has no date. There is a black dragon on a background of red and yellow diagonal stripes. The organisers had run out of medals by the time I finished, so they had to scrounge around for mine. This one was left over from the previous year's stock.

They were terribly embarrassed, and two weeks after the race, posted me the real thing with a letter of apology. I phoned the race director and told her it was fine. It was a hard-fought prize and they need not have gone to all that trouble.

London awarded a chucky item. The reverse of the medal has a picture of the Tower of London in bold relief. On the front is a logo of a person finishing across a tape, with the 2004 date bar. The ribbon is colourful too: green, yellow, red and blue vertical stripes.

The medal from New Zealand is not made of bronze like the first two, but of a grey metal alloy. It was the fortieth running of the race, so the medal was made in the shape of the number. The zero is distorted to resemble the shape of the lake Rotorua. The ribbon is plain red. On the reverse it says "Rotorua Marathon — New Zealand. Finisher 1st May 2004".

Of all of the medals on my bookcase, the one I prize the most is from the Rio Marathon. It was so hard-fought. I know my time for that race was by far the slowest, but not many can boast a 2004 Rio Marathon finish. It is rather thin by comparison, but it is silver and grotesquely large. There is a graphic of the two mountains that make up the Sugar Loaf, such an icon of the city.

When I passed through customs, the officials spotted a large metallic object in my hand luggage. Opening the zip the official dug out my medal. On the front in Portuguese it states "Maratona Caixa da cidade do Rio de Janeiro 2004".

"Ah, you — you win this?"

"Yes."

"This is good — okay you can go." A smile as large as Sugar Loaf.

Soon after I got back home, I pinned an Olympic lapel badge on the royal blue ribbon. This was in recognition of Vanderlei de Lima of Brazil. This race taught me how to overcome adversity, and the medal has a special place in my collection.

The Hong Kong Marathon medal is monstrous. It has no ribbon and it is huge, silver and opens like a book. This is so you can put a photograph in it. I look at this medal with disappointment, if not scorn. Hong Kong was a hard-fought race. I had to beat five hours, and I did this after a serious bout of hepatitis.

What upset me was that the medal was handed out in our

goodie bags before the race. I felt cheated. A medal is awarded for achieving a standard, crossing a threshold, not for pitching up at registration. There is honour among runners though, and I know that if I had not made the cut, I would have thrown the medal away. On the front in bold relief in both English and Chinese it says "Hong Kong Marathon 2005".

The North American medal is a heavy bronze affair with a white guitar on the front. "Country Music Marathon — April 30, 2005, Nashville". It is considered quite an achievement to run a marathon in America. A young man came up to me when I had finished and asked if he could be photographed with my medal. "Did you run the race?" I asked. "No, but it is a life's ambition and I just want to hold your medal."

"Well okay then, I will take the photo but here is the condition. You are not allowed to put the medal around your neck, only hold it."

"Oh, why?"

"Honour among athletes. You will understand this one day when you finish your first big race."

In the picture he holds the medal in his hand, grinning from ear to ear. As I took the shot I thought: "Hopes and dreams — that is what this is all about — and a little bit of truth."

On my bookcase is a small piece of broken glass, a reminder of unfinished business in Antarctica.

The material content of my quest comes down to six medals, nineteen stones and six T-shirts. I have six running numbers and a few airline stubs. Not much to show for such a large conversation.

Tonight I take one stone from each continent. I hold them in my hand and shut my eyes. There is magic and power here. I hold the world in my hand. Great wisdom in my palm. That wisdom is contained in all the stories and conversations of many generations, from an entire planet. Now I know that I am but a speck of dust in the blink of time. But ah, for that one moment in that timeless marathon race, I became the very heartbeat of the Universal Runner.

A handful of stones: a simple and ordinary thing. But ah, there is a conversation there.

* * *

I sit at the dining room table. It is winter. There is a friendly glow coming from the anthracite stove in the passage. I have made the fire, and I have tended to it with a mindfulness that makes Master Sen smile. All present in the Renoir print on the wall reflect the warmth and intimacy of those in the room.

Around the table, glasses are charged and Charles Aznavour sings softly in the background. I feel extraordinarily powerful emotions — a deep love for those present. I feel that same love for myself. I set out with serious intent to find that part of me that I knew existed, and I found even more than I hoped for.

I have come full circle. I started this journey at this table, and here it ends. I have two parcels for my daughters, gifts that I wish to share with them both. I try to fight the tears, but they come so easily and so freely. I need to close this quest with an important symbolic act of faith. In silence I sit, with my head bowed. Patiently, lovingly, my family waits.

I lift my head, and struggle with words that are so difficult to find. One by one the travellers, companions and guides come into view in the Oregon orange glow and the shadows made by the candlelight.

Inyathi steps forward and silently touches his forehead in acknowledgement. "Makos, *Yebonga* my lord, thank you. I see you now Great Buffalo. You were my teacher and I am honoured to have been your student. I will never fear again. My family will grow strong for a thousand years. I am One with this world and with the next."

Zeno steps forward, and bows slightly. Our eyes meet. "Thank you my father, for teaching me more than I will ever know." Zeno acknowledges me. "You were a worthy student. Guard carefully your thoughts; keep your mind from becoming polluted."

It is the turn of Taina, the Maori youth. Hands folded across his chest, proud, warrior-like. "Hey Pakeha, our performances were heroic on that day, your *hau* is still with us on our island, it shall always be there, always your wind will be with us."

Silvia, the guide from Ipanema. "Ola Tomas, old friend. Your work is your art. Your wealth is not counted in what you have, but by how little you need. Oh, and for the wine at your table, *obrigado*, my friend."

Then it is the turn of Sen, the samurai warrior. With one hand on his sword, he bows forward slightly and points to his eye. "Focus. That is all it takes. You ran a brave race my student. You have done well."

Lame Deer steps forward. "Your deep love comes from all who are around you. Cherish your people, be of service to your community."

Scott Seaward. "Ah fuck man ... Ah shit Tom, you got another glass of wine there? It's fucking cold outside."

Next to him a man with a wise presence. "Who knows, Tom, if this is good luck?" Jed.

Each interaction took less than a second, and yet each lasted an eternity. There is a strength and a presence in this room. Each is a fellow pilgrim, a guide and a teacher. They were always part of me and I am evermore part of them. I am the sum total of my guides, in this life and beyond.

I rise and hand each daughter the parcel I have carefully wrapped. In it are the pages of this book. I try to make a speech, but I cannot speak. I sit and allow the tears to flow. This is perhaps the largest love letter any father could write to his children, but then brevity was never my style. They each know what the parcel contains and they accept this gift with an equal amount of love.

The music softly plays in the background. "Happy Anniversary ..." Aznavour croons. I look at Kay and know that our love will last longer than time ...

"Well this is Terry Jack of Sporttime Radio. We have followed this remarkable runner to every corner of the world, and watched in amazement his slow, ponderous and useless running, tell me Tom ..."

"Ah fuck off, Terry."

"Well this is Terry Jack signing off, thank you for being such patient and interested listeners. Join me next week when we will meet a mountain climber who has been to every continent and has climbed the highest peak on each. Remember, sport is the name of our game, and goodnight."

* * *

Could I ever be so vain to think that people will boast that they lived in the time of Tom Cottrell? What an epic life one would have to live for future generations to carry such a boast.

It is more than enough if my children say, "He was my father". More than enough if my wife one day says, "I was married to Tom Cottrell". If these people say these words with love, pride and dignity, my pilgrimage would not have been in vain. If even one person is inspired to go on their own personal pilgrimage, then the philosophical meanderings of this nobody would be worthwhile.

For the man, the "b-teamer", the "b-streamer", the one who never gets the chicks. For the girl, the large one in the G-team, keeping goal. For all those who secretly wish they were more whole. I shall whisper to you in the breaking of the dawn. You can find the courage to make your own pilgrimage. Embark on your own epic.

For all the heroes who catch the bus to work every day. For those who weep at night for a lost love, or fear for the future. For those who gaze with wonder and awe at their young children or rejoice at the first rains of summer. For those heroes — those of life — it is time for your journey.

RUN THE MARATHON OF HOPE AND TRUTH WITH TOM COTTRELL

Learn how to find your *own* balance, focus and direction

Multi-disciplined Tom Cottrell has trained and coached many of Johannesburg's top professionals to achieve a life of health and fitness. He has also trained the full spectrum of athletes, from the nervous and hopeful novice, to a Comrades Marathon champion.

His motivational talks to a wide variety of Comrades Marathon runners, both novice and seasoned, as well as non-runners, are inspirational. A skilled and sensitive Hospice counsellor, Tom deeply understands the human condition, and regularly gives talks on what *really* matters.

Tom has written a story of wisdom and power — *Five Hour Pilgrim* — that will change your definition of personal success forever. Join the masterful writer and coach on a day-long seminar to learn the practical wisdom of "Hope and Truth". The seminar includes teas, lunch and a signed copy of the *Five Hour Pilgrim*. You will also take away a personal workbook with practical, workable solutions to apply to your own life.

Tom conducts a seminar once a month and classes are limited to twenty delegates, so early booking is essential.

For further details or to book call Ann or Tom on 011-646-9760, or email *tom@runnersguide.co.za*. Group seminars and in-house corporate seminars by arrangement.